WALKING

LAKELAN
Keswick & the North

Paul Hannon

HILLSIDE

HILLSIDE GUIDES - ACROSS THE NORTH & BEYOND

The Uplands of Britain
- THE HIGH PEAKS OF ENGLAND & WALES
- YORKSHIRE DALES, MOORS & FELLS

Long Distance Walks
- COAST TO COAST WALK
- DALES WAY
- CLEVELAND WAY
- WESTMORLAND WAY
- FURNESS WAY
- CUMBRIA WAY
- BRONTE WAY
- PENDLE WAY
- NIDDERDALE WAY
- LADY ANNE'S WAY
- TRANS-PENNINE WAY
- CALDERDALE WAY

Hillwalking - Lake District
- LAKELAND FELLS - SOUTH
- LAKELAND FELLS - EAST
- LAKELAND FELLS - NORTH
- LAKELAND FELLS - WEST

Circular Walks - Peak District
- NORTHERN PEAK
- EASTERN PEAK
- CENTRAL PEAK
- SOUTHERN PEAK
- WESTERN PEAK

Circular Walks - Yorkshire Dales
- HOWGILL FELLS
- THREE PEAKS
- MALHAMDALE
- WHARFEDALE
- NIDDERDALE
- WENSLEYDALE
- SWALEDALE
- HARROGATE & WHARFE VALLEY
- RIPON & LOWER WENSLEYDALE

Circular Walks - North York Moors
- WESTERN MOORS
- SOUTHERN MOORS
- HOWARDIAN HILLS

Circular Walks - South Pennines
- BRONTE COUNTRY
- ILKLEY MOOR
- CALDERDALE
- SOUTHERN PENNINES

Circular Walks - Lancashire/North West
- BOWLAND
- PENDLE & THE RIBBLE
- WEST PENNINE MOORS
- ARNSIDE & SILVERDALE

Circular Walks - North Pennines
- TEESDALE
- EDEN VALLEY
- ALSTON & ALLENDALE

Waymaster Guides - Short Scenic Walks
- WHARFEDALE
- AMBLESIDE & LANGDALE

- AIRE VALLEY BIKING GUIDE
- CALDERDALE BIKING GUIDE
- WHARFEDALE BIKING GUIDE

- YORK WALKS *City Theme Walks*

Send for a detailed current catalogue and pricelist

LAKELAND FELLS
Keswick & the North

JOHN·RUSKIN·:

·MDCCCXIX + MDCCCC·:

Paul Hannon

HILLSIDE

HILLSIDE
PUBLICATIONS
20 Wheathead Crescent
Keighley
West Yorkshire
BD22 6LX

First published 1998
3rd Impression 2008

© Paul Hannon 1998, 2008

ISBN   978 1 870141 62 8

Cover illustration: On Causey Pike, looking to Skiddaw
Back cover: Derwentwater from Grange Fell;
Robinson from Newlands; Grisedale Pike from under Skiddaw
(Paul Hannon/Hillslides Picture Library)

Page 1: Bannerdale Crags from the River Glenderamackin
Page 3: Ruskin Memorial, Friar's Crag

The sketch maps are based upon 1947 Ordnance Survey 1" maps

Printed in Great Britain by
Carnmor Print
95-97 London Road
Preston
Lancashire
PR1 4BA

CONTENTS

INTRODUCTION

The fells of the Lake District are the most impressive and most popular in England. The majority of the National Park's 866 square miles is dominated by its hills, from the rocky fastnesses of Scafell Pike, the summit of England, down to some delightful low-level fells. To do justice to this unique landscape, 100 outstanding fellwalks have been devised and shared among a series of four definitive guidebooks. Together these embrace the best fellwalking in the country, and each guide deals with a logically defined area of Lakeland.

The walks within this volume cover the northern part of the National Park, with Keswick as the focal point. Other popular bases are Borrowdale and Newlands, and some of the best known fells include Blencathra, Causey Pike, Skiddaw and Catbells. The three companion guides feature Ambleside & the South; Patterdale & the East; and Buttermere & the West.

Although any number of more demanding walks can be planned by enthusiasts, the aim of this series is to provide a varied range of outings within the scope of most walkers. Thus a limit of around 10 miles and 3500 feet of ascent per walk has been set: most walks are in fact well within these bounds. A feature of these walks is their variety, so that ridgewalks alternate with valley approaches, there are steep climbs, gentle climbs, routes that include mountain tarns and waterfalls. All share the character that makes the Lakeland Fells so special.

The great majority of the Lakeland Fells is freely open to walkers, though many of the routes described are in any case on public rights of way. Any access routes onto the hills are always on rights of way or permitted routes. Please be sensitive when passing near farms and dwellings, and if you must take a dog with you, ensure it is on a lead. While we may have every right to be there, the sheer weight of our numbers means it is particularly important to also act responsibly.

Mountain safety is a subject dealt with in several chunky volumes, and here it should be sufficient to say that the most important elements are to be properly equipped, and realistically aware of the three great limitations of time, physical condition and weather. An ability to use map and compass is strongly recommended, as one can be easily disorientated in mist. In winter conditions the fells take on an entirely different character. In such circumstances even the humblest of fells present new dangers: ice, snow, bitterly cold or gale force winds, and

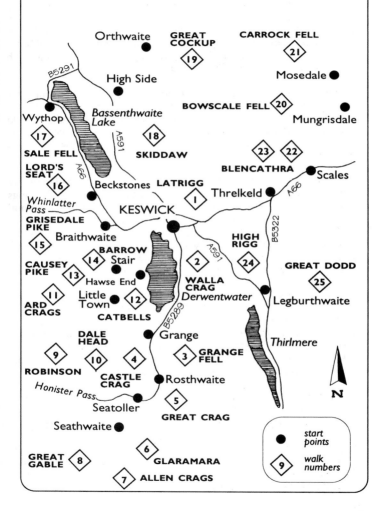

WALKING COUNTRY - LAKELAND FELLS NORTH

Orthwaite

GREAT COCKUP ⟨19⟩

CARROCK FELL ⟨21⟩

B5291

High Side

Mosedale

Bassenthwaite Lake

BOWSCALE FELL ⟨20⟩

Wythop ⟨17⟩

Mungrisdale

SALE FELL

A591

⟨18⟩

LORD'S SEAT ⟨16⟩

SKIDDAW

⟨23⟩ ⟨22⟩

BLENCATHRA

Scales

A66

Beckstones

LATRIGG

Whinlatter Pass

A66

KESWICK ⟨1⟩ Threlkeld

GRISEDALE PIKE ⟨15⟩ Braithwaite

HIGH RIGG ⟨24⟩

B5322

BARROW ⟨14⟩ Stair

⟨2⟩

A591

GREAT DODD ⟨25⟩

CAUSEY PIKE ⟨13⟩ Hawse End

WALLA CRAG

Derwentwater

ARD CRAGS ⟨11⟩ Little Town

⟨12⟩

Legburthwaite

CATBELLS

DALE HEAD ⟨10⟩ Grange

B5289

⟨9⟩

⟨4⟩

⟨3⟩ **GRANGE FELL**

Thirlmere

ROBINSON

CASTLE CRAG Rosthwaite

Honister Pass

⟨5⟩

N

Seatoller

GREAT CRAG

Seathwaite

GREAT GABLE ⟨8⟩

⟨6⟩ **GLARAMARA**

⟨7⟩ **ALLEN CRAGS**

● *start points*

⟨9⟩ *walk numbers*

short daylight hours all demand greater preparation. In true winter conditions one should carry ice axe and crampons and be competent in their use. Don't be put off the winter experience, however, for it is in this season that the fells are seen at their most stunningly beautiful.

The overwhelming popularity of these hills is all too evident to those who set foot upon them. Many paths are worn wide and bare, and in most parts of the district evidence of repair work will be encountered. In recent years this has grown into a major undertaking, with the National Park and the National Trust at the forefront. In most cases the paths are sensitively restored with stone surfaces, a dramatic improvement on the ugly scars they replace. Wherever possible please adhere to the paths old and new, and to any diversions during ongoing pathwork. Additionally, walkers can show respect for our fragile hills by faithfully following zigzags and avoiding insensitive short-cuts; not descending at speed; not walking the fells in enormous groups; and by wearing the lightest footwear that doesn't jeopardise safety.

Most of the walks begin from villages or recognised parking areas, but please be sure not to obstruct local access. Many walks can also be accessed by public transport, so even if you came to the district by car, consider the local bus whenever possible in order not to exacerbate peak season traffic congestion. Stagecoach Cumberland produces an annual timetable which includes numerous seasonal services.

Using the guide
Each walk is self-contained, featuring essential details, sketch map, and route description including comment on features along the way. The basic maps serve merely to identify the location of the routes, for which a 1:25,000 scale map is strongly recommended. Best known for their excellent detail are the Ordnance Survey Outdoor Leisure maps, of which four cover the Lake District (1998 editions onward):-
4 - *English Lakes North West*   5 - *English Lakes North East*
6 - *English Lakes South West*   7 - *English Lakes South East*
(walks in this guide are on 4 and 5, and one briefly overlaps onto 6)

Useful for general planning purposes are the Landranger maps at 1:50,000, and just one sheet covers the area:
90 - Penrith, Keswick & Ambleside

The increasingly popular Harvey Maps also cover the district, and their 1:25,000 scale Superwalker maps are available as follows:
*North West Lakeland   Western Lakeland   Northern Lakeland
Eastern Lakeland   Southern Lakeland   Central Lakeland*

SOME USEFUL ADDRESSES

Ramblers' Association
2nd Floor, Camelford House, 87-89 Albert Embankment, London SE1 7BR
Tel. 020-7339 8500

Lake District National Park Visitor Centre
Brockhole, Windermere (on A591)   Tel. 015394-46601

National Park/Tourist Information
Moot Hall, Market Square, **Keswick**   Tel. 017687-72645
Seatoller Barn, **Seatoller**   Tel. 017687-77294
Town Hall, Market Street, **Cockermouth**   Tel. 01900-822634
Penrith Museum, Middlegate, **Penrith**   Tel. 01768-867466

Public Transport
Traveline - Tel. 0870-608 2608
National Rail Enquiries - Tel. 08457-484950

Lake District Weatherline - Tel. 017687-75757

Lake District National Park Authority
Murley Moss, Oxenholme Rd, Kendal LA9 7RL Tel. 01539-724555

Cumbria Tourist Board
Ashleigh, Holly Road, Windermere LA23 2AQ   Tel. 015394-44444

Friends of the Lake District
Murley Moss, Kendal LA9 7SS   Tel. 01539-720788

The National Trust North West Regional Office
The Hollens, Grasmere, Ambleside LA22 9QZ   Tel. 0870-609 5391

The Country Code
- Respect the life and work of the countryside
- Protect wildlife, plants and trees
- Keep to public paths across farmland
- Safeguard water supplies
- Go carefully on country roads
- Keep dogs under control ● Guard against all risks of fire
- Fasten all gates ● Leave no litter - take it with you
- Make no unnecessary noise
- Leave livestock, crops and machinery alone
- Use gates and stiles to cross fences, hedges and walls

SUMMITS	
LATRIGG	1207ft/368m

START Keswick　　　　　　　　**Grid ref.** NY 266234

DISTANCE 6 miles/9½km　　　**ASCENT** 900ft/275m

ORDNANCE SURVEY MAPS
1:50,000 - Landranger 89 **or** 90　　　1:25,000 - Outdoor Leisure 4

ACCESS *Start from the Market Place. There are several central car parks. Keswick is served by bus from all surrounding towns.*

Latrigg is a low grassy wedge, a sibling of Skiddaw yet far removed from that lofty peak. It occupies little space on the ground, yet hovers importantly over the streets of Keswick and offers a magical half-day ramble when Skiddaw and its kind appear overfacing.

S　　Leave the Moot Hall in the Market Place by way of St. John's Street, Station Street and Station Road, and once across the river turn left into Fitz Park. Crossing to the far corner, an urban footpath escapes to emerge onto the back road of Brundholme Road at a dismantled railway bridge. Turn right a short distance, with Latrigg 'towering' directly above, and the Skiddaw massif to its left. Quickly strike off on Spooney Green Lane opposite the houses of Briar Rigg, climbing to bridge the by-pass in a scene inconceivable not that very long ago.

Sanity is restored as the track climbs past Thorny Plats and up by a plantation. The steepness soon relents, never to return. Opportunities to strike out more positively for Latrigg's summit soon present themselves with regularity, but they should all be refused in favour of the main highway with its views across to Skiddaw beyond open gorse banks: sections of both Bassenthwaite Lake and Derwentwater can be seen, while the north-western fells are well displayed, dominated by the graceful cone of Grisedale Pike.

After woodland on the left ends, the path swings out into more open country, heading directly away from our goal. Just beyond though, a dark, extensive plantation adjoins the path, and for this short spell there is a curious absence of any views. The broad path is finally vacated well along the plantation, opting for a more inviting green path that doubles back to the right. In the tradition of this ascent it zigzags famously up through receding bracken with the ease of an escalator - now it is clear why we waited for it! With the western end of what constitutes Latrigg's summit ridge underfoot, Keswick lies outspread below, though the picture of Derwentwater and Borrowdale beyond is a big improvement on the streets and roofs of the town.

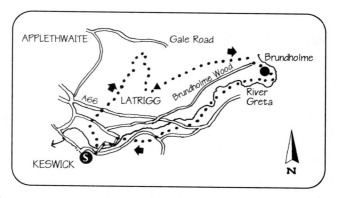

A substantial mound now leads up to the felltop, which has no cairn and is decidedly arbitrary but nevertheless thoroughly wonderful. Latrigg's summit is exposed and windswept, but with two or three hardy trees nearby. Just below, the top end of a newer plantation only just fails to reach the top. Looking to the north, the Skiddaw massif appears a world away in both height and bulk.

Continuing along the edge, the mound runs along to its demise at a fence, and from the stile there a green path commences a gradual descent of Latrigg's east ridge. A long way further it is deflected left to join a green track, which is the continuation of the Gale Road that ends its surfaced life on the northern slope of Latrigg. This takes over to continue down the ridge, with super views of the colourful Glenderaterra Valley in front, backed by Blencathra. The track descends through gorse to a junction of back roads. Two alternative returns are offered here, both by way of Brundholme Woods. The right branch, a minor road, is the most direct, while just before it a permissive path remains on the flank of the fell to run more attractively through the woods. The road curving round to the left leads only to Lonscale Farm.

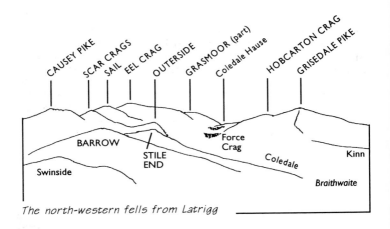

The north-western fells from Latrigg

Instead, go left a few yards and take the road descending past Brundholme to an arched bridge over Glenderaterra Beck. Without crossing the bridge, a short path runs to the old Penrith-Keswick railway line, which provides a novel return to the start. Turning right, it commences a remarkable journey through the wooded gorge of the river Greta, crossing the tumbling waters on several occasions and providing alternatives that head off into the woods. The old track bed was purchased and transformed into a walkers' route by the National Park Authority, but even their imaginative efforts couldn't cope with the intrusion of the Keswick by-pass. Just beyond the caravans at the former bobbin mill at Briery (note the old platform), a rare and spectacular viewpoint opens out, looking upstream towards Blencathra, and straight across the river to the steep flanks of Latrigg.

This point marks a brief departure, not from the line, but of the line. The embankment of the by-pass has obliterated the course of the railway, and a climb to the edge of the pulsating highway is an alarming moment prior to the realisation that it doesn't have to be crossed. The path runs down to the right to pass under the road at the commencement of its sweeping concrete crossing high above the Greta. So often a jarring note in views across the Vale of Keswick, here it is experienced in the mind-numbing flesh. Awe-inspiring it may be, but it is also probably the most horrendous sight in the entire National Park.

On the other side the track bed returns, suddenly now very much on the urban edge of Keswick. It nevertheless gives an interesting route into town, passing under the main road and then back over the road and adjacent river to chug into the restored station. Closed in 1972, one can eat, drink, and obtain timeshare information here. In view of the demise of the Cockermouth, Keswick & Penrith Railway this tarting up seems incongruous; insulting even, by the time a sign pointing to a 'brasserie' is reached. To return to the centre turn left in front of the swimming pool to drop down onto Station Road, and follow this back up between the parks.

The Moot Hall,
Market Place, Keswick

> ### SUMMITS
> *WALLA CRAG   1243ft/379m*

START *Keswick*   **Grid ref.** *NY 263228*

DISTANCE *5½ miles/9km*   **ASCENT** *1050ft/320m*

ORDNANCE SURVEY MAPS
1:50,000 - Landranger 89 or 90   *1:25,000 - Outdoor Leisure 4*

ACCESS *Start from Derwentwater boat landings. The Lakeside car park is nearby. Keswick is served by bus from all surrounding towns.*

A hugely entertaining ramble that combines a wealth of features above the lovely wooded shores of Derwentwater.

S   From the boat landings immediately forsake the lakeside road in favour of a path into the woodland just past the National Trust kiosk. There turn right along a wide path curving round through Cockshot Wood, emerging at the other side to run between fields out onto the Borrowdale road. Straight across, a gate gives access to Castlehead Wood, first rising steeply towards a brow before a branch up to the right to the crown of Castle Head. Curiously, Castle Head itself is not named on the Outdoor Leisure map.

A mere 531ft/162m above sea level, this is arguably Derwentwater's finest viewpoint, certainly for the modest effort involved. High above the lake to the left is the brooding frame of Walla Crag, looking far larger than it really is, and belying the ease by which its top will be gained. Returning to the path junction continue along to the right, descending to the edge of what is in season a glorious bluebell wood, and out along another enclosed path onto Springs Road.

Turn right along Springs Road, with Walla Crag on the skyline ahead. This suburban row leads to Springs Farm, where bear left on a path that climbs above the wooded charms of Brockle Beck. The first good views out look over Derwentwater to the Borrowdale and Newlands Fells. At the top the beck is crossed by a footbridge to rise onto a narrow lane. Go right to its imminent demise at Rakefoot, keeping right at the fork where Walla Crag earns its own roadsign. A small footbridge re-crosses the beck to a path climbing by the wall-side, and through a stile the open fell is reached.

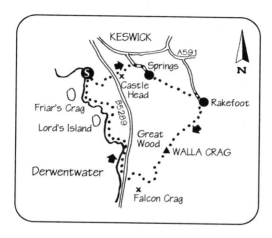

Remaining near the wall throughout, it is but a gentle grassy pull onto Walla Crag. The drama unfolds rapidly as the main path crosses the wall at a kissing-gate, to cautiously follow the edge of the clifftops. Leaving the last of the trees the path runs to a cairn standing on the highest point, just yards back from the alarmingly abrupt escarpment. The breathtaking panorama over the expanse of Derwentwater is guaranteed to demand a substantial break in the journey.

All of interest is contained within the small package of land between the wall and the cliff. Slabs of rock pave much of the higher ground, with a stand of hardy juniper only yards to the north. Few will tarry long by the cairn, for eyes will first be fixed on the bird's-eye picture of Derwentwater and the valley floor beyond Great Wood, then progress naturally to that stately grouping of mountains across the water. So breathtaking is the scene from the cragtops that it may be wise to nail youngsters to the ground to allay fears of them straying near the edge.

From the summit resume along the path heading south, which within a couple of minutes re-crosses the wall at a stile. Continue down by the wall on a short-cropped green carpet, with the Jaws of Borrowdale leading the eye to the mountains at the dalehead. The path undergoes a drastic character change as the environs of Cat Gill, with its fine waterfalls, are entered. The ground steepens rapidly and the path begins a winding descent towards the Borrowdale road, with much essential restoration work having rendered the path more bearable.

At the foot of the steeper section Great Wood is entered, to leave it again by way of a footbridge over the beck, near the bottom. Back out on bracken-cloaked lower slopes, a level path heads away to appraise the mighty cliff of Falcon Crag up to the left, a favourite haunt of rock climbers. Beneath the first main crag a green path doubles back down to the right to a stile onto the road, which can be crossed straight over to Derwentwater's shore.

Turning right along the lakeshore, a finish that does justice to the rest of the walk is now in store. In and out of woodland the path curves round Calfclose Bay, being diverted briefly away from the lake by the house at Stable Hills. Following its drive away, at the first opportunity it is escaped on a well trodden path to the left to run through trees. The shore is regained in time to reach the famous peninsula of Friar's Crag (see illustration on page 3), from where it is but a few hundred heavily populated yards back to the boat landings, and the ice cream, and the ducks, and ....

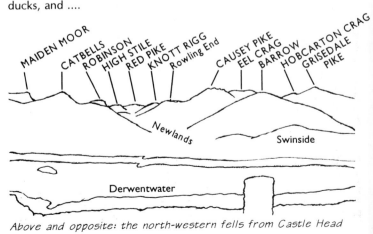

Above and opposite: the north-western fells from Castle Head

16

```
            SUMMITS
  KING'S HOW    1286ft/392m
  BRUND FELL    1363ft/415m
```

START Grange in Borrowdale   **Grid ref.** NY 253173

DISTANCE 6 miles/9½km   **ASCENT** 1420ft/433m

ORDNANCE SURVEY MAPS
1:50,000 - Landranger 89 **or** 90   1:25,000 - Outdoor Leisure 4

ACCESS Start from Grange Bridge, alongside the B5289 Borrowdale road. There is limited parking space at the bridge end, with laybys on the main road towards Keswick (on the route). Served by Keswick-Seatoller buses.

This ungainly wedge of upland encompasses all that is special about the Lake District, and about Borrowdale in particular. Crags, woodland, bracken and heather together form a rich mixture, the latter being especially regally draped over much of the higher part of the fell. Come to explore Grange Fell on a summer's day, and salute the high mountains from a heathery couch!

S Leave Grange by crossing the famous double-arched bridge over the Derwent and turning right along the main road. Just beyond the large house a stile admits to the bracken-clad fell, and a path heads away. Keeping left it rises through scattered birchwoods with frowning crags above. A broader green way joins from the right and the path rises to a brow, then through a bridle-gate and down to a fork. Ignoring the left branch to a stile, the right arm drops down to cross a tiny stream to begin a long climb through the beautifully wooded slopes of King's How, westernmost and lower of Grange Fell's two principal tops.

Occasional glimpses of Derwentwater can be stolen while pausing on this largely rebuilt path, then suddenly the going eases and the work is done. The path runs along towards a fence, but instead of crossing it at the stile, rises alongside it to the edge of Long Moss, between heathery knolls. King's How rises immediately across it. Skirting the moss to the right the path meanders a little to a corner above the main valley, then begins the final short climb. This presents panoramic views into Borrowdale, with a glimpse of Grange itself before the last pull to the scattered summit cairn. Just below the highest point an easily missed tablet affixed to the rock records in fine words the gift of King's How to the nation.

> In Loving Memory of King Edward VII Grange Fell is dedicated by his sister Louise as a sanctuary of rest and peace. Here may all beings gather strength, and find in scenes of beautiful nature a cause for gratitude and love to God giving them courage and vigour to carry on his will.

This is the higher of the two fells known by many as the 'Jaws of Borrowdale', for along with Castle Crag (see WALK 4) it forces the Derwent and the parallel road through a narrow wooded defile between the upper valley and Derwentwater.

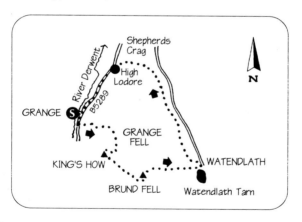

To the south-east Brund Fell, true summit of Grange Fell makes its superiority clear. To reach it, retrace steps a few yards to the tiny cairned saddle just below the monument, and take the path to the right. It drops steeply to skirt the top end of Long Moss to the fence which can finally be crossed. The path continues on past a ruin to an intervening wall, and shortly after a steep rise beyond a ruined sheepfold, a branch bearing up to the left is taken. Here the path from Rosthwaite is joined for the final climb onto the summit. The highest of several rocky tors is crowned by a cairn: while this top has much more interest than King's How, it forfeits the magnificent view of Derwentwater.

The main path off the top maintains the direction of the ascent, winding down north-eastwards to a stile in the nearby wall corner. Head directly away to the east, bearing left on a faint path that joins the wall there for a descent to Watendlath that conceals the tarn and its environs almost until the very last minute. On crossing the outflow of a large marsh on a shelf, the path contours round above the wall to finally reveal, and in some style just in front, the delectable Watendlath scene. A short drop to a kissing-gate leads down to join the Rosthwaite bridleway just short of the outflow of the tarn.

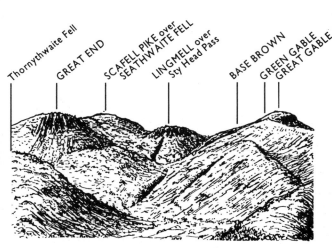

The Seathwaite skyline from Grange Fell

With refreshments usually available this is a charming place for a potter about, and on leaving it is necessary to re-cross the bridge to a gate adjacent to it. After only a few yards in the company of the lively Watendlath Beck, the path is ushered away by a wall to run through the level Watendlath Valley along the base of Grange Fell. In time the water's edge is rejoined, and a lovely stroll concludes in glorious woodland at a footbridge.

Without crossing the bridge, go left to a kissing-gate into the edge of Ashness Wood. When the beck is briefly encountered again, simply turn downstream above a ferociously thundering fall through a gorge. The path then advances straight on to a collapsed wall on a grassy saddle. From here a short detour can easily be made along the path to the right, which rises onto the colourful top of Shepherds Crag, Grange Fell's final salute. This is a near island of rock, and has an excellent view of Gowder Crag across the now deep rift of Watendlath Beck.

Back at the saddle, with Borrowdale laid out in front, the path makes the short descent of Ladder Brow to return to the valley by way of High Lodore Farm (more refreshments). Turning left, the roadside footpath past the *Borrowdale Hotel* affords a reasonable means of returning to Grange, and a short final section takes to the riverbank.

At Watendlath

SUMMITS
CASTLE CRAG   951ft/290m

START *Grange in Borrowdale*   **Grid ref.** *NY 253173*

DISTANCE *4 miles/6½km*   **ASCENT** *750ft/228m*

ORDNANCE SURVEY MAPS
*1:50,000 - Landranger 89 **or** 90*   *1:25,000 - Outdoor Leisure 4*

ACCESS *Start from Grange Bridge, alongside the B5289 Borrowdale road. There is limited parking space at the bridge end, with laybys on the main road towards Keswick. Served by Keswick-Seatoller buses.*

A volcanic upthrust unwittingly created one of the gems of the district, and Castle Crag is a prime example of the old adage that size isn't everything. Its modest stature is a positive advantage given its position, for in Lakeland's most beautiful valley this is a perfect eminence from which to appreciate both the charms of the dale and still gain a perspective of the surrounding mountains.

S Leave Grange by a lane heading south out of the village centre, this being the drive to Hollows Farm and bridleway (old road) to Honister and Seatoller. Level walking leads to a junction, just before which Castle Crag reveals itself ahead as a wooded knoll. Here the Hollows Farm road swings right, and a wide track continues into the woods to join the Derwent. After the second of two footbridges on inflowing streams, a guidepost signals the point to leave the river and take the right fork. Steady climbing now begins, on the wide track of the old road to Honister. Rise with the stream, soon crossing it and breaking out into more open country between woodland and fellside.

As height is gained the lofty Goat Crag on High Spy and Castle Crag's own impressive cliffs form mighty portals. The stream is re-crossed, and as the scree on the left recedes the brow of the old road is approached. Before re-crossing to the right bank of the stream a massive cairn on the grass signifies the point of departure, by curving up to the top of a small tor on the left. Here will be found a stile in a wall, and a clear path climbs steeply past a memorial seat and tablet and up to another wall-stile at the foot of scree slopes.

Here are the remains of a slate quarry, and the main path bears right, spiralling up to a cairn at the bottom of a vast spoil heap. It is to this point that steps must be retraced after reaching the summit. A firmly trodden path zigzags up the mountain of slate in surprisingly easy fashion, to arrive at a platform with slate cairns overlooking an exquisite panorama of upper Borrowdale. Behind them is the surprisingly extensive quarry site, with the path climbing to its right to gain the grassy summit plateau.

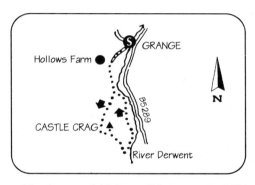

The most striking feature of this incredibly interesting hill is the sudden view revealed to the north, where the waters of the Derwent glide past the white-walled houses of Grange, leading the eye to Derwentwater backed by Skiddaw and a host of lower fells. The highest point is in no doubt, a great cairn sat atop a large mound of rock to which is affixed a memorial tablet, with the lip of the quarry encroaching dangerously close. While savouring this classic summit, it can easily be envisaged as the ancient British hillfort it once was. A more fitting location could not exist for a memorial to the Borrowdale men lost in the Great War.

On regaining the foot of the great spoil heap cross the grass to the nearest stile over the adjacent wall, and from it take the path down to the left. It quickly returns to valley level to meet and then turn left with a broad, level path. Almost at once entering thick woodland to follow the Derwent, a walk in heaven ensues. Although remaining generally close to the river, the main path turns off part-way along, and at a junction just past a gateway and spoil heaps there is an opportunity for a short detour up to the left to inspect caves once occupied by one of the district's great characters, Millican Dalton. During the first half of the 20th century, this educated if somewhat eccentric chap made this quarried hole his summer home, enjoying a leisurely life in these beautiful surroundings: amongst his numerous interests he acted as an informal mountain guide.

This point can also be reached by a lesser known path that keeps faith with the river longer, being partly a wide green swathe and partly an obstacle course of ponds and outcrops, a veritable wonderland. The main path can be regained by leaving the river at a rock-bound impasse, and turning inland up a curious trough to the spoil heaps at the foot of the caves. Beyond here the re-united path eventually returns to the crystal clear river to rejoin the outward route at the wide bend where it was earlier forsaken. An easy stroll leads back to Grange and its various refreshments.

Grange in Borrowdale:
The River Derwent, with High Spy behind

24

```
            SUMMITS
GREAT CRAG    1496ft/456m
```

START Rosthwaite   **Grid ref.** NY 258148

DISTANCE 5 miles/8km   **ASCENT** 1450ft/442m

ORDNANCE SURVEY MAPS
1:50,000 - Landranger 89 **or** 90   1:25,000 - Outdoor Leisure 4

ACCESS Start from the village centre. There is a small car park. Served by bus from Keswick.

Great Crag is a rather anonymous, retiring fell, yet is a fascinating tract of upland that offers much to the explorer. This complete line of ascent from valley level packs much into such little space: riverside stroll, steep ascent, beautiful woodland, lively beck, heather moorland, secluded tarn, and airy summit.

S From the Post office head north a few yards along the road then take the lane that turns off to cross a bridge on Stonethwaite Beck. Here the beck is of similar proportions to, and often mistaken for, the Derwent which it will shortly swell. Immediately across, turn right along an old walled lane, a beautiful walk between woodland and the beck. Shortly after passing the bridge leading to Stonethwaite across the beck, the path emerges into more open country at a well maintained sheepfold. The scene ahead is dominated by the fine outline of Eagle Crag. Advance a little further along the walled way, and after a gateway take a thinner path rising left up the wallside, into the trees.

Almost at once a steep climb ensues, and a magnificently constructed stone path spirals endlessly up through the oakwood. Above the trees the going eases abruptly for a well earned break on a knoll beneath a ruin. The long awaited views out feature a good picture of the upper Borrowdale scene, including Eagle Crag, Sergeant's Crag, Rosthwaite

Fell, Glaramara, and Honister Crag above Seatoller. Now the path runs up through heather above the ravine of Willygrass Gill. Beyond a wall-stile closer acquaintance is made with the more subdued upper section of the beck as it is shadowed up to the outlet of Dock Tarn.

The path continues along the bank of the tarn, in a colourful setting amid a tangle of rocks and heather. Shortly after the end of the tarn, a gap in the heather-clad knolls on the left reveals the elusive summit of Great Crag, its cairned top being surprisingly close beyond one of the countless hollows. A thin path winds between the knolls, and on becoming fainter simply strike up onto the summit, being the first (southernmost) of two neighbouring cairned tops. It would be a shame to rush over Great Crag, for exploring its many surprising corners is a major part of its attraction.

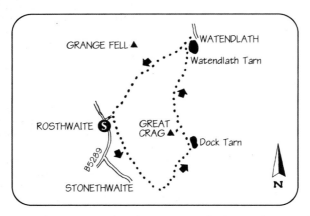

Great Crag boasts a privileged position in the heart of Borrowdale, where only the more glamorous 'Jaws of Borrowdale' can match this lovely situation. In stark contrast to the slimline pastures of Stonethwaite and the richly wooded lower flanks, the hinterland of the summit is a tangled upland, seen at its best when the heather blooms in late summer. Across the silvery waters of Dock Tarn, the fell's ill-defined boundary merges with that of Ullscarf's extensive, sprawling flanks: beyond, the long Helvellyn ridge forms the skyline. While the view may be dominated by the Lakeland giants across the head of Borrowdale, nothing can equal the cameo moment as Watendlath Tarn and its hamlet are revealed exactly as the cairn is touched.

The lower north top enjoys a fuller view of the Watendlath scene, and both this and the saddle between the tops send paths dropping back down to regain the main path. Once on it, the path continues its course to Watendlath by descending steeply to a kissing-gate in a sturdy wall. Immediately beyond, it crosses a moist enclosure on a re-routed path indicated by a line of stakes. A little before reaching the far corner, the option of making a more direct return to Rosthwaite can be taken up by forking left when the stakes indicate such a junction: this branch heads left to a gate in a fence, then heads away along the broad ridge of the fell to gain the Rosthwaite-Watendlath bridleway just west of its summit.

The suggested route advances to the corner of the marshy enclosure, then descends in the company of a small stream. On crossing it there are a few pathless yards to the left before a track forms to quickly become enclosed. This attractive walled lane is followed pleasurably past Watendlath Tarn to the hamlet at its outflow, nestling in its idyllic upland bowl. With refreshments usually available and a generally endearing nature, this is a delightful place to sojourn before the final section of the walk. The return to Rosthwaite commences at the point where the walled lane emerges at the tarn foot.

The broad path climbing the fellside is a time-honoured route, and the rise to its summit from Watendlath is but a simple stroll. A nice level section precedes the more prolonged descent to Borrowdale, which is delightful all the way with its truly beautiful views over the main valley to the high mountains at the dalehead. The white-walled cottages of Rosthwaite appear and a briefly steeper drop leads through scattered trees. The valley floor is reached at the bridge over Stonethwaite Beck where the walk began, so retrace those first steps to finish.

Eagle Crag
from the path by
Stonethwaite Beck

GLARAMARA

SUMMITS
GLARAMARA 2569ft/783m
DOVENEST TOP 2073ft/632m

START Seatoller

Grid ref. NY 244137

DISTANCE 6½ miles/10½km

ASCENT 2510ft/765m

ORDNANCE SURVEY MAPS
1:50,000 - Landranger 89 **or** 90   1:25,000 - Outdoor Leisure 4

ACCESS Start from the centre of the hamlet. There is a National Trust car park. Served by bus from Keswick.

Glaramara is a connoisseur's fell, full of interest and favourably sited at the head of one of Lakeland's busiest valleys. Its great bulk is an integral part of the Borrowdale scene, with exceedingly colourful lower slopes; steep, often rough, flanks; and bags of character on top. It demands - and deserves - to be climbed.

Key to this walk is Combe Gill, which from a hidden entrance drives a deep incision into Glaramara's northern flank, cradled by the walk's two broad ridges. The staircase of Thornythwaite Fell offers a traditional line of ascent, while the high-level return route is a hugely absorbing experience.

S Leave Seatoller by a stile at the end of the car park. Heading away, keep right at an initial fork and the path runs on into woodland. Emerging from the trees to a gateway, take the right branch down to a prominent stone arched bridge on the deep, clear Derwent. Cross the fieldside with a good prospect ahead to Combe Gill sandwiched between the walk's two ridges. The valley road is joined at the houses at Mountain View. Cross straight over and along Thorneythwaite farm drive. Take an early stile on the left and a path rises up the mixed pasture, joining a farm track to continue up with a wall on the left. It swings to shadow Combe Gill over the wall, and rises to a kissing-gate.

Tumbling waterfalls lead the way into Combe Gill's secret amphitheatre, where the grey Raven Crag towers ahead and the enclosing arms of the ridges confine one's horizons. With a sheepfold across the beck (which the return leg will pass), advance to a cairn just ahead. This heralds a fork, as the main path starts its climb away from the beck. This well worn path scales the flank of Thornythwaite Fell, gradually revealing more of the great basin of Combe Gill under the wall of Raven Crag. The path finally gains the ridgetop proper, a grand moment which opens up views west including the sharp profile of Honister Crag.

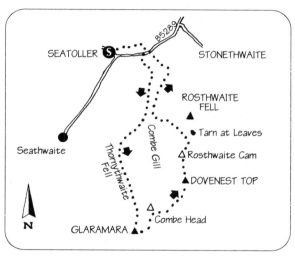

The path scales the ridge at a steady angle, soon gaining a knoll (point 574m) where a level section is reached. From here on the climb becomes gentler still, as the path rises to the base of the summit crags. An easy scramble breaches the crags to gain the summit in sporting fashion, though if deterred go right (west) to circumvent the crags. Glaramara's broad summit is decorated by twin-like outcrops each with its own cairn. The traditional top is found just up to the right, marked by a fine cairn, though the true summit is a little further southwest across a saddle. As already experienced, the view northwards over Borrowdale is superb, now joined more comprehensively by the array of high peaks at the very heart of Lakeland: the pairing of Great Gable overtopping its sidekick Green Gable is particularly good.

The return route is a splendid, intriguing walk, but can be tiresome, and potentially dangerous in poor visibility. In such conditions the less experienced might wisely opt for an easier onward route, either returning the same way, or turning to the descent route to Seathwaite as used in WALK 7. Also, allow ample time for the full return.

Descent begins from the north-east top, above the cliffs. Leave by heading south-east to avoid the crags, down grassy slopes between small outcrops. A thin path forms, and suddenly turns down to the left through the last of the crags, indicated by a couple of cairns. It then winds a sinuous course across a gentle marsh around the back of Combe Head, suddenly facing a steep drop to a tarn in a marshy hollow. A short, clear descent to this reveals Combe Door on the left, offering a steep descent to the head of Combe Gill. Passing to the right of the tarn, a fainter rise leads to the minor top immediately behind. Revealed ahead is the next summit, Dovenest Top, further identified by the rough flank of Cam Crag on its eastern side.

Take care departing the scrappy cairn as the immediate northern flank is very rough: angle more to the right to descend an improving little path to some pools on a shelf. Continue down to and across a saddle, passing a small pool on the left at the start of the easy rise onto Dovenest Top. At the path's highest point on a little col, a trod rises left for half a minute to the bare rib of rock that makes a superb summit. This is also known as Dovenest Crag, though that title is potentially confusing as Dovenest Crag itself is some way down the western flank, in Combe Gill.

Ahead, the solid rock boss of Rosthwaite Cam appears across the void of Great Hollow. Other features of the view include the floor of Langstrath down to the right, backed by Eagle Crag and Sergeant's Crag, while Derwentwater is seen to the north over Grange Fell. Leave by resuming north, through a little rock cutting and enjoying a steady amble down to the marshy hollow. The path bears left across this, its apparently errant meanderings proving to be the best approach to the short pull onto Rosthwaite Cam.

The path runs through a gap alongside the Cam, which will take some missing by anyone traversing the ridge. On gaining it is is found to be one almighty boulder offering a variety of scrambling routes, the easiest being little more than a walk onto its top. From here eyes are first drawn, inevitably on this ridgewalk, to the next stage along, and this proves to be the last one, as Tarn at Leaves reposes in a hollow beneath the spiky top of Bessyboot. Other features of the view include Seatoller, Honister Crag, Crummock Water over Honister Pass, and a good portion of Borrowdale. Indeed, this is as good a viewpoint as any for the whole route.

A nice steady descent towards Tarn at Leaves leads to a hollow just short of it. Here bear left to find a good path forming within a matter of yards, just past the beginnings of Rottenstone Gill. It slants neatly across the flank away from the gill, then winds faintly down the easy slopes. Odd zigzags can be traced as the sheepfold near the outward path in Combe Gill appears below. Keeping short of Dry Gill, some old grassy grooves make a clearer conclusion leading the way down to the fold.

Turn downstream to a gate in the descending wall at a sheepfold, and a smashing green path heads away through the bracken. It runs largely level for some time, as far as a guidepost above an old mill by the beck. This sends the path branching left down to an access track by an attractive stone arched bridge. Visible upstream is the mill which used to grind the local corn, and it still retains a rusting iron waterwheel. The route meanwhile concludes by crossing the bridge and following the track out onto the road. Turn left to finish, either as the walk began, or simply by following the road back into Seatoller.

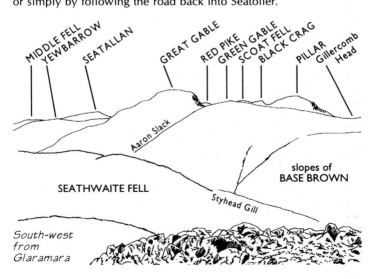

South-west from Glaramara

ALLEN CRAGS

```
SUMMITS
ALLEN CRAGS    2575ft/785m
GLARAMARA SOUTH TOP    2365ft/721m
GLARAMARA    2569ft/783m
```

START Seathwaite   **Grid ref.** NY 235121

DISTANCE 6 miles/9½km   **ASCENT** 2855ft/870m

ORDNANCE SURVEY MAPS
1:50,000 - Landranger 89 **or** 90   1:25,000 - Outdoor Leisure 4 & 6

ACCESS Start from the road-end at Seathwaite, a mile off the B5289 at Seatoller. Roadside parking on the verge approaching the farm. Seatoller is served by bus from Keswick.

A good climb on a restored path leads to Esk Hause, hub of the district, from where a classic high level walk is a succession of delights, encountering rocky tops and mountain tarns in abundance.

S Seathwaite is departed through the farmyard and out on a broad track to soon make closer acquaintance with the river Derwent. Ahead rises the abrupt end of Seathwaite Fell, with our return skyline walk up to the left. The gushing spout of Taylorgill Force makes a splendid sight on Styhead Gill across the valley. Beyond the meeting of Styhead Gill and Grains Gill to form the Derwent, the latter is crossed at the lovely arch of Stockley Bridge. Through the gate behind, the Sty Head traffic is escaped by turning left on the wallside path up the valley of Grains Gill.

Very easy walking high above the wooded ravine leads to a small footbridge on a smaller ravine, on what is now the main beck, Ruddy Gill. The climbing begins in earnest now as the restored path shadows the beck up narrowing confines. On turning a corner the upper reaches of Ruddy Gill are revealed, its ravine providing colourful company as the path climbs to a sharp bend in it, with the rugged slopes of Great End in front. Dropping down to cross this bend the path rises to join the broad Sty Head-Esk Hause path. Rise left on it, still with the ravine in attendance, and a fork in the ravine coincides with a major fork in the path. With Allen Crags in front, take the lower left-hand one to resume a steady rise onto Esk Hause. A cairn presides over a T-junction of paths. The venerable cross-wall shelter is found less than 100 yards to the right.

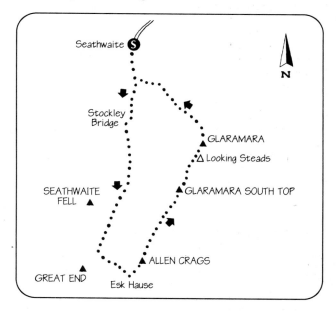

Esk Hause is a great meeting place of walkers' steps, and though this staggered crossroads is the focal point, the true Esk Hause is in fact 100ft higher, on the col between Esk Pike and Great End, to the south. Without advancing to the shelter, the route turns sharp left at the cairned junction, and the twin summit cairns of Allen Crags will be alongside within minutes.

Allen Crags is a fell in the engine room of the district, and not surprisingly provides extensive views in which the Grasmoor and Skiddaw groups are ranged above Borrowdale and Derwentwater. Attention, however, is likely to be hi-jacked by the giants in close attendance: Bowfell, Esk Pike, Great End and Great Gable, of which Great End appears particularly bold, and the Gables, rather more detached across the trench of Sty Head, positively resplendent.

From Allen Crags the bulk of Glaramara looms large along the ridge, and a clear path links the two in splendid fashion. The traverse begins with a steady descent, then skirting left around a minor top (point 684m) which deserves a visit. This attractive cairned top looks down on Lincomb Tarns in the next saddle, and also back to reveal Sprinkling Tarn on its Seathwaite Fell shelf, backed by Great Gable. Descending, the most interesting route visits a stunning tarn on a rocky shelf. This lovely pool was described by Wainwright as the 'perfect mountain tarn', and it offers an interesting exercise in a full circumnavigation - easier done clockwise.

The saddle below it holds Lincomb Tarns and High House Tarn, where the main path can be rejoined to the left. Re-ascending, a steady rise passes a small tarn on another shelf to gain the summit of Glaramara's South Top. This time the path crosses the very crest, which features cairns on the rocky spine to both left and right. The final saddle holds a reedy pool on the right, before another steady climb towards the minor top of Looking Steads (2543ft/775m). The path circles well to the left of its flat top to approach Glaramara's summit.

Glaramara's broad summit is decorated by twin-like outcrops each with its own cairn. Uncertain as to the highest point, the path climbs directly to the true summit in front, but also branches right to the north-east top. The highest summit is reached first, a less dramatic top than the slightly lower traditional one, which is found just across a saddle to the north-east. This is marked by a fine cairn on a rocky knoll, perched above a more substantial craggy drop to the north. As already experienced, the array of high peaks at the very heart of Lakeland is all-embracing: the pairing of Great Gable overtopping its sidekick Green Gable is particularly good. Now more comprehensively re-vealed however is the superb view northwards down through the Jaws of Borrowdale, leading the eye to Derwentwater backed as ever by trusty Skiddaw.

Though not today's route, the ridge running north from the summit is the more traditional route of descent, a good path running along the crest of Thornythwaite Fell and directly down to Combe Gill for Seatoller via Mountain View. This walk, however, takes a lesser known descent to Seathwaite. From either top begin by locating the saddle between them, and despite being profusely cairned, only a thin grassy trod descends steadily to the western rim of the felltop. Here more cairns tempt one across the embryo Hind Gill and attendant marshy tract to continue along the ridge, when in fact the required route turns left before the beck. With no more cairns nor even a thin trod, it hesitantly sets off over the grassy edge. The valley floor quickly appears, as does the spout of Taylorgill Force beneath the Gables. Remaining close to the beck a thin trod soon resurrects itself, as do the cairns a little farther down, each being tidily perched on a boulder.

As the white-walled buildings of Seathwaite come into view far below, the slope steepens, the cairns increase and the path suddenly becomes very clear. This steep section does not last unduly long, and lower down it brings the reward of smashing glimpses into a now substantial ravine bedecked with colourful vegetation. At a gate in the intake wall the gradient eases, and though the path loses itself by the beck it matters not as the valley bottom is just ahead. At the bottom of the pasture the beck is crossed to a gate giving access to the track on which the walk commenced, just short of Seathwaite.

Stockley Bridge

SUMMITS	
BASE BROWN	2119ft/646m
GREEN GABLE	2628ft/801m
GREAT GABLE	2949ft/899m

START Seathwaite   **Grid ref.** NY 235121

DISTANCE 5½ miles/9km   **ASCENT** 2855ft/870m

ORDNANCE SURVEY MAPS
1:50,000 - Landranger 89 **or** 90   1:25,000 - Outdoor Leisure 4

ACCESS Start from the road-end at Seathwaite, a mile off the B5289 at Seatoller. Roadside parking on the verge approaching the farm. Seatoller is served by bus from Keswick.

A celebrated pilgrimage to one of Lakeland's favourite sons, using two splendid approach fells as high-level stepping-stones.

S Pass into the farmyard and turn immediately right under the farm buildings, where an enclosed way runs along to a footbridge on the river Derwent. The peak of Base Brown towers immediately above, but even more impending is the prospect of the climb by Sourmilk Gill. A largely rebuilt stairway displays miraculous restoration work, where unsightly scars have been replaced with a near-permanent stone bed. This direct assault enjoys a very entertaining climb with a brief hands-on section and good views of the waterslides.

At the top the path runs left to a gate in a sturdy wall, and then rises more gently. The beck is rejoined briefly for a final waterfall, then the going eases out and the built path ends upon arrival at the rim of the hanging valley of Gillercomb. Directly across is the mighty Raven Crag, better known to climbers as Gillercomb Buttress. The direct path runs a very clear course across the basin before climbing to the valley head, but far more rewarding is the inclusion, for very little extra effort, of Base Brown. This carries the double bonus of neatly breaking up the climbing and also escaping the crowds.

Now on the level, leave the path and strike left up grassy slopes towards the nose-end of the fell, aiming for the base of the skyline crag. As the going steepens a massive boulder is passed to find a level path running beneath the crag. Turn left on it beneath the now unmissable perched boulder of the Hanging Stone, also enjoying a bird's-eye view of the Seathwaite scene. Within yards the crag abates to permit a simple clamber over easy-angled slabs, but the path continues a little further for an even easier slant back up. Either way, all that remains is a steady rise on a generally thin but clear path up the broad, easing rise to the summit.

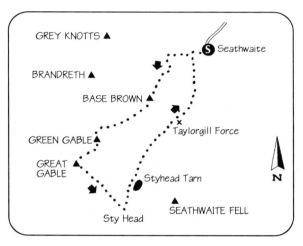

The cairn appears backed by Green Gable, itself overtopped by the upper contours of Great Gable. Base Brown's location among the high fells but in the pocket of one valley leaves it with an unbalanced view, though the good bits are very good. The Scafells are ranged splendidly across the gulf of Sty Head, with Lingmell seamed by the ravine of Piers Gill; Black Crag flaunts a hugely impressive profile to the left of Pillar, while the cliff of Gillercomb Buttress on Grey Knotts excites across Gillercomb.

Leave by resuming the direction to the Gables, a thin and very gentle path running along down to rejoin the main path at a grassy col. A steady rise past an overkill of cairns leads to the main ridge, where the path from Honister Pass is joined. New revelations to the west now include Crummock Water and the shapely Grasmoor group of fells. In the company of a ridiculous number of cairns turn left for the final few minutes' climb onto the top of Green Gable. This is a stunning moment as the parent fell appears in all its glory, the awesome prospect of mighty Gable Crag looming quite intimidatingly: brilliant stuff!

Green Gable, though underling of internationally renowned Great Gable is in truth a worthy fell in itself: its status is not diminished by the imposing presence of big brother, but merely by its own inability to assert itself more effectively above the aptly named divide of Windy Gap. Green Gable's summit is a pleasant, lofty perch, and diverting eyes from Gable Crag it has much else to offer. The fell is of sufficient altitude to add the delights of the Buttermere Valley to what is probably the most complete view of Ennerdale's upper miles, watched over by an impressive Pillar.

Green Gable and Great Gable from Black Sail Hut,
at the head of Ennerdale

38

A five minute descent through dusty red scree has the slim defile of Windy Gap underfoot, during which time Styhead Tarn appears below. The ensuing final pull onto Great Gable is the walk's roughest section, a rocky clamber up above Gable Crag onto the stony summit dome. At the top a few easier strides are lead by the inevitable cairns across the boulder-strewn felltop to one of Lakeland's favourite summits. On touching the highest rock, a final reward is the memorable appearance of Wastwater, set deep in its trench of fells and leading the eye to the Irish Sea.

Great Gable shares with Scafell Pike an attraction for people who would normally never dream of venturing up a high mountain. This speaks volumes for the high regard in which it is held, for no-one can deny its magnetism. No other mountain in Lakeland so draws the eye, nor exerts such a mystical influence on the walker in the valley below. The summit is a characterful place, the highest feet occupied by a final upthrust of rock, and a plaque records the gift of this and surrounding fells to the nation in memory of members of the Fell & Rock Climbing Club who gave their lives in the Great War: a remembrance service is conducted here each November.

If the summit be busy then the discerning walker will flee the scene, and within two minutes be reposing alongside the Westmorland Cairn to the south, as often as not in complete solitude. The fact that it is out of sight of the summit is as welcome as the experience it provides. This precariously balanced edifice is a famous landmark, its virtues as a viewpoint self-evident as it overlooks the deep trough of Wastwater. As might be expected the complete summit panorama is absolutely superb, but the Scafell massif will always demand most attention.

Leave by heading east on a cairned and immediately clear path. This descends an easy stony course to a mini rock gateway, where the path swings briefly right across a shelf. Here is the start of an award-winning rebuilt path, a mammoth effort completed in 1995. Unstable slopes of eroded scree have been arrested by the building of a near-permanent stone path for the entire remaining descent to Sty Head. In addition to protecting the mountain, it has to be said the firmly set stones also afford a very easy passage. When Sty Head and its tarn do appear they still seem a long way down, but the boulder and attendant stretcher box are reached with ease as the path leads directly to the crest of one of the best known foot passes in the district.

Turn left **here** on the path running down past the shore of Styhead Tarn, very much a place to linger with the work all but done. A little downstream a footbridge is reached beneath Patterson's Fold. The main path crosses and resumes downstream, dropping down to Stockley Bridge and then left along the valley floor back to Seathwaite.

Immensely more interesting is the path remaining on the west bank. This descends, largely free from humanity, above the beck to approach the wooded environs of Taylorgill Force. The great plume of the falls is soon revealed from a super viewpoint, and the path then sets off on a spirited traverse across a scree slope beneath Base Brown's craggy flank. A brief hands-on section sees the path down to a gate, a cracking final viewpoint for the falls. Easier going then leads into pastures through which the path runs unfailingly back to the start, passing above a small plantation then beneath another. Between the two look up to see the Hanging Rock 'hanging' directly above! The last stage sees the youthful Derwent leading the path back to the footbridge where the climb began.

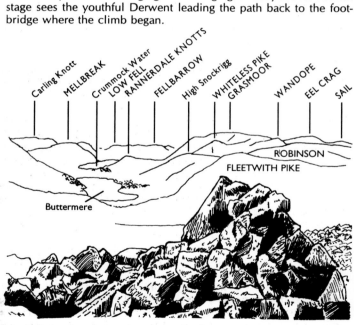

The Buttermere Valley from Moses' Trod, under Green Gable

SUMMITS	
ROBINSON	2418ft/737m
HINDSCARTH	2385ft/727m

START Little Town, Newlands

Grid ref. NY 232194

DISTANCE 6½ miles/10½km

ASCENT 2460ft/750m

ORDNANCE SURVEY MAPS
1:50,000 - Landranger 89 **or** 90   1:25,000 - Outdoor Leisure 4

ACCESS Start from Chapel Bridge, just south of Little Town. There is a car park on the east side of the bridge.

This pair of peaks pose great appeal in their shapely aspects from the Newlands area, and their twin-like northern ridges combine to form a connoisseurs' outing from that delectable vale.

S Chapel Bridge is left by the road to the west, which is itself left within yards on a narrow road to Newlands church. Attached to it is the even tinier Newlands school, closed in 1967. Keeping right, a surfaced lane climbs to the farm at Low High Snab. Here a path takes over to soon break out onto the open fell as an inviting green way. At the first opportunity a broad path breaks off right for a direct climb through bracken to gain the ridge of High Snab Bank. This is a super moment as the already superb Newlands views are joined by the prospect of the shapely ridges of the Grasmoor group to the west.

The ridge rapidly narrows into a classic route before starting to gain height in earnest. A couple of miniature scrambles up rock slabs above Blea Crags precede a longer but splendid pull above the rim of Robinson Crags. At a cairn that promised to be the highest, the true summit is easily gained over gentler terrain, the final strides being long ones over short turf. The summit is flat and quite extensive, and along with a fine array of fells, various sheets of water in the Buttermere Valley are on display - with one notable absentee.

Across the hanging valley of Little Dale to the east rises the whaleback of Hindscarth, and a horseshoe walk commences on a path south to join a fence that runs above the Gatesgarth escarpment to Littledale Edge. At the col a direct path breaks off to slant up to Hindscarth's broad summit, but fades towards the end. The better way is to remain on the main path as it rises to the southern end of Hindscarth's summit ridge, where the main ridge continues to Dale Head. From this crest fork left for a gentle skyline walk to Hindscarth's summit cairn, which doubles as a shelter.

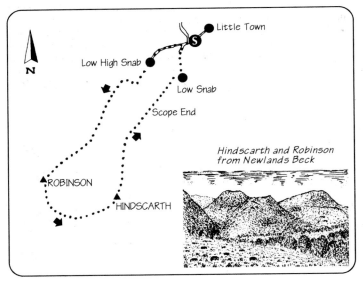

Hindscarth and Robinson from Newlands Beck

This central peak on the ridge linking Honister Pass and Newlands Hause stands aloof from its neighbours, its summit sitting back from the watershed and shunning the Buttermere Valley in favour of Newlands. The view is good but is bettered by those that are gone and are still to come. There are good prospects of the High Stile and Grasmoor groups; and interesting aspects of Eagle Crag, above Greenup, and Yewbarrow slotting in over Black Sail Pass.

Less than two hundred yards to the north of the summit a great, sprawling shelter cairn brings Newlands back into the scene, and marks the commencement of the descent. An initially steep section is

42

helped by some agreeable zigzags, below which a gentler stroll leads towards the ridge of Scope End. The first stage shuns the ridgetop in favour of the eastern flank, an airy little traverse that precedes even finer walking along the narrow, heathery crest of Scope End. With glorious views, this is a quite enchanting amble before a lively descent of the ridge-end encounters innumerable playful miniature rock barriers.

At the intake wall and fence the path drops down to the right above Low Snab Farm to arrive at the spoil heaps of the former Goldscope Mine. A choice of finishes awaits. First option is to drop down with the farm track and down the wallside to a footbridge on Newlands Beck, joining an old mine road to go left, where just short of Little Town a short-cut path drops to a stile onto the road just above Chapel Bridge. Alternatively and more directly, take the gate into the farm (a permissive route), passing straight through the yard and out along the drive back to Newlands Church.

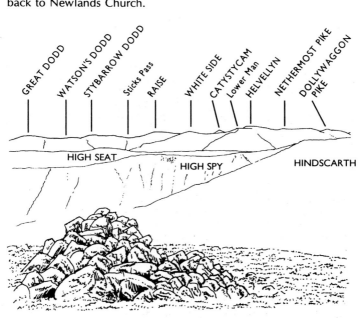

On Robinson, looking east to the Helvellyn range

SUMMITS
DALE HEAD   2470ft/753m
HIGH SPY   2142ft/653m
MAIDEN MOOR   1889ft/576m

START Little Town, Newlands

Grid ref. NY 232194

DISTANCE 7 miles/11km

ASCENT 2575ft/785m

ORDNANCE SURVEY MAPS
1:50,000 - Landranger 89 **or** 90   1:25,000 - Outdoor Leisure 4

ACCESS Start from Chapel Bridge, just south of Little Town. There is a car park on the east side of the bridge.

A splendid ramble around the upper reaches of the Newlands Valley, linking a seldom trodden ascent route with an easy, panoramic return.

S Head briefly back up the road towards Little Town, but at the first chance take a stile on the right, from where a rebuilt path climbs onto a broad track. This former mine road leads along the base of the fell to the right, bound for the upper Newlands Valley. Ahead are Dale Head, set back, and the more shapely Hindscarth to its right. When the attendant wall parts company, with the former Goldscope leadmines prominent across the beck, keep straight on the track. Our line of ascent for now looks less than obvious amid the shadowy north face of Dale Head, but all will soon fall into place.

A wall returns and leads past a climbing hut to the spur of Castle Nook and the remains of the Castlenook Mine. Turning the corner behind it, the upper part of the dalehead is revealed featuring the depression of Dalehead Tarn, while up to the left scree and much vegetation decorate Eel Crags on High Spy's flank. Within a couple of minutes the path forks. The left branch begins its climb to Dalehead Tarn, offering a useful short-cut on a good path if wishing to omit Dale Head.

The main route, however, takes the inviting green track straight ahead to quickly join the beck. Remain on its bank to the end of the marsh opposite, where solid stepping-stones lead to the other bank. Slant left to cross the sidestream of Near Tongue Gill, and trace it up to the foot of a steeper section. At this point a grassy, grooved way is seen slanting invitingly up to the left, and this is the way to go. Initially steep, it is however a pleasant, seldom trodden route created by miners of old. Occasional rests will allow time to survey the magnificent dalehead surrounds, including a smashing waterfall across on the infant Newlands Beck; views down the valley lead to Causey Pike and Skiddaw.

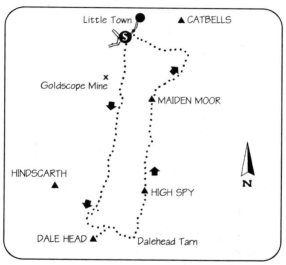

Ultimately the path breaks journey to cross Far Tongue Gill beneath a splendid ravine. Rising again with the sombre Gable Crag ('Great Gable' on the OS map) in front, the old way then engages a series of mercurial zigzags to emerge onto a bouldery shelf. This is the site of the Dale Head Mine, where copper was won. A faint 100 yards lead to a ruin, beyond which the nature of the path changes as it winds up the steeper slope behind.

Surprisingly, the steeper section quickly eases and the path angles up to the left, becoming ever easier as it slants further left above Gable Crag, enjoying a splendid traverse to emerge onto a knoll on the eastern shoulder of the fell, and joins the well worn direct path from Dalehead Tarn. This is another fine moment, revealing an attractive cameo of the white-walled cottages of Rosthwaite amid Borrowdale's green fields; and a skyline including the Langdale Pikes, Glaramara, Bowfell and Esk Pike. Though the route is to descend this path after visiting Dale Head's summit, for now turn uphill for the few short minutes to gain the top.

The summit cairn perches airily above the rim, with Newlands Beck leading the eye to the familiar Skiddaw grouping: a glimpse into the void will explain the mountain's name. Even the cairn is rather special, suggesting its slates were gelled by craftsmen from its old quarries above Honister Crag. The summit yields one of Lakeland's finest views, successfully fusing a rare variety of features: a precipitous drop, a tinkling beck (Newlands), extensive cliffs (Eel Crags on High Spy), a green valley (lower Newlands), a lake (Bassenthwaite, just), and a plethora of distinct mountain groupings headed by Helvellyn, Grasmoor, the Scafells and Gable/Pillar.

Having come this far, it is worth a near level two-minute stroll west along the ridge path to bring a large chunk of Buttermere into the scene, giving further perspective to the imposing High Stile ridge. Indeed, one could opt to continue along Hindscarth Edge and return over Hindscarth, as in WALK 9. To the north-east, meanwhile, across Newlands Beck, High Spy awaits above the riven wall of Eel Crags. The way onto this mountain involves a descent eastwards to Dalehead Tarn. Retrace steps above the steep edge back to the knoll where we recently emerged. Below this point, the path strikes more directly down to Dalehead Tarn, much of it on a rebuilt section. The path passes alongside the tarn's north shore at an old sheepfold, this little corner offering itself as a perfect place for a break.

The path forges on to drop down to meet the circuitous course of the tarn's outflow. After crossing, a direct return to the head of Newlands starts faintly on the left, but the main path unhurriedly sets about the knobbly flank of High Spy. The going is undemanding throughout, becoming ever gentler until the cairn appears just 50 yards in front. This solid summit cairn hovers only yards from the brink. Though not a famous name, High Spy has more than its share of attributes. The western face boasts the mile-long precipice of Eel Crags, a forbidding grey wall beneath which the lonely headwaters of Newlands Beck are a stark contrast to the relative bustle of Borrowdale.

Leave the top by resuming north for a super stroll, with tantalising glimpses down the cliffs of Eel Crags, and parts of Derwentwater and Bassenthwaite Lake appearing ahead. A gentle drop through a saddle leads to the north top. Descending from here Derwentwater appears in an immense way, and continuing north the path crosses aptly named Narrow Moor. On departing it the path divides for half a mile, the main path across Maiden Moor giving the summit a wide berth. Opt instead for the slimmer left fork, which keeps Newlands in view while crossing the heathery top to a scrappy cairn. While the void of Newlands will always offer the most dramatic scenes, with the ridges of Hindscarth and Robinson climbing in distinguished fashion to their respective summits, there is also an appealing glimpse to the giants of Scafell Pike, Scafell and Great Gable slotting neatly into the saddle of Dalehead Tarn.

From its highest point the path is forced north-east by a craggy flank, with little Catbells suddenly looking a shapely character ahead. Rejoining the other arm brings a super picture of upper Borrowdale and the Stonethwaite Valley. A glorious descent of the ridge is now enjoyed high above Derwentwater and its rich surround of woodland. At the saddle of Hause Gate the descent is concluded by restoring allegiance to Newlands on a path slanting down to the left. Arriving above old mine workings a cairn sends a more direct branch down to the left, descending through the spoil at the heart of the former Yewthwaite Mine. The path continues down to merge into a broad track running along the base of the fell. Go left briefly to approach the cluster of white-walled dwellings at Little Town. Joining the road here, Church Bridge is just down to the left.

On Dale Head,
looking to
High Spy and
a distant
Skiddaw

ARD CRAGS

```
              SUMMITS
   ARD CRAGS   1906ft/581m
   KNOTT RIGG  1824ft/556m
```

START Little Town, Newlands

Grid ref. NY 232194

DISTANCE 6½ miles/10½km

ASCENT 1706ft/520m

ORDNANCE SURVEY MAPS
1:50,000 - Landranger 89 **or** 90   1:25,000 - Outdoor Leisure 4

ACCESS Start from Chapel Bridge, just south of Little Town. There is a car park on the east side of the bridge. An alternative start is Rigg Beck, where the Braithwaite-Buttermere road meets a hairpin bend (parking area in an old quarry by the bridge, grid ref. NY 229201).

A classic 'mini' fellwalk of airy ridges and rich views.

S From the car park cross the bridge and take the narrow, winding road rising away. Ahead, Causey Pike dominates things, with the pairing of Hindscarth and Robinson looking superb over to the left. The Newlands Pass road is joined at Rigg Beck. The house here is in its own inimitable way a Lakeland landmark, and it looks down on a hairpin bend where the road crosses the beck. Cross the bridge and take an inviting path along its right bank. Up to the right is the serrated top of Causey Pike, but very quickly the noble outline of Ard Crags proves equally arresting across the beck. When the wall turns away up the opposite slope, descend to cross the beck and do likewise.

A steep little pull leads onto the broad spur, and a faint trod bears right along it. At the base of this eye-catching profile, a clear green path begins the climb through bracken. Heather takes over on the steeper, winding path, which meets a sudden halt and well-earned respite on the crest of Aikin Knott. After a few level strides a shorter pull through the heather gains the elongated summit ridge. A glorious walk now leads along an exquisite ridge to the tiny summit cairn on Ard Crags.

Ard Crags is the highest point of this curving ridge running from Newlands Hause to the Newlands Valley, in the shadow of a ridge reaching a thousand feet higher yet travelling a similar course. While the imposing eastern faces of Eel Crag and its neighbours present a majestic sight, they take nothing away from the delights of Ard Crags' heathery crest. The airy summit stands directly above the col of Rigg Pass, where a speedy move to the higher ridge could be effected.

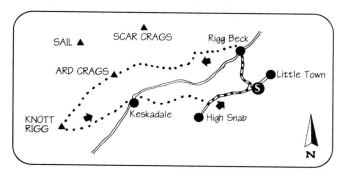

A sensational plunge of gullies from the other side of the summit adds impact to this magnificent viewpoint, and its modest altitude amid superior heights makes it a perfect viewing platform. Great Gable makes its familiar presence felt in front of the Scafells, and Pillar stands suitably tall above High Crag. A nice glimpse into the Buttermere Valley narrowly fails to locate either of its lakes, but Sourmilk Gill makes a fine centrepiece to High Stile and Red Pike. It is left to Derwentwater to provide the only lake scenery, and even this is no more than has been visible for much of the climb.

The path continues along the crest for the natural progression to Knott Rigg, immediately encountering the head of a gully falling dramatically to Keskadale. In the minor depression grass takes over for the steady rise onto Knott Rigg's less exhilarating summit, the highest point of this trusty sidekick of Ard Crags being set some distance back. During this crossing the route of descent down Keskadale Edge will be readily appraised.

Having savoured the views over Newlands Pass to the Buttermere Valley, double sharply back left across a small marshy area (note the fenced-off bogs). This brings arrival at the head of the side valley of Ill

Gill, enclosed by the protective arm of Keskadale Edge. Bearing right of it a thin path materialises to commence a descent of the extremely well-defined edge. The descent over its mainly heathery undulations is utter delight, a miniature classic to be taken at a leisurely pace. At the foot of the edge bear down to the left to join the road just below Keskadale Farm.

After doubling back left to cross Ill Gill, leave the road by a gate on the right, from where a track runs down with the beck to a farm bridge and then a footbridge over Ill Gill and Keskadale Beck respectively. Rising left, the intermittent track fades after pointing the way up the bank over to the left. Bear left above the bank of the beck to a small footbridge, and a fence leads away to pass beneath a compact birchwood. Several of these pastures are liable to feature some rather moist sections. At the end slant right over a minor brow, then take a direct line through stiles linking several pastures to join the farm road beneath High Snab. Turning down it, lonely Newlands church will be passed just before the junction at Chapel Bridge.

Ard Crags from Rigg Beck

```
                    SUMMITS
        CATBELLS    1480ft/451m
```

START Hawse End   **Grid ref.** NY 247212

DISTANCE 3 miles/5km   **ASCENT** 1150ft/350m

ORDNANCE SURVEY MAPS
1:50,000 - Landranger 89 **or** 90   1:25,000 - Outdoor Leisure 4

ACCESS Start from the Portinscale-Grange road at Hawse End on the western shore of Derwentwater. There is car parking below the cattle-grid by the zigzags, and a car park just along the farm road to Skelgill. Hawse End landing, ten minutes away, is served by motor launch from Keswick.

Of the Lakeland fells that attract as many casual walkers as fellwalkers, shapeliest and best known is Catbells. Its enviable position on the shore of Derwentwater is such that anyone in Keswick with stout legs and a sense of adventure cannot fail to be drawn to it. Very little description is needed for this popular stroll, which utilises only some of the delectable paths around Catbells. Of all the walks in this book, reserve this one for Autumn.

S From the junction above the cattle-grid turn along the narrow road to Skelgill, past the car park. This initial stage is dominated by the arresting profile of Causey Pike across the valley. Continue above the hamlet on a broad track along the base of the fell. The Newlands Valley now fully unfolds, an unforgettable picture centred on the shapely peak of Hindscarth.

A good two-thirds of a mile beyond Skelgill the first of two paths breaks off to the left, directly beneath the summit crags. This outstand-ing green way runs virtually parallel for some time, but eventually curves above Brunt Crag and Yewthwaite Mine, the very evident remains of a former lead mine. This old green way absorbs a path

51

climbing through the mine from Little Town before the final short pull to Hause Gate, which is Catbells' link with Maiden Moor and the higher fells to the south. This is a truly mouth-watering moment as Derwentwater bursts onto the scene in a big way, backed by fine wooded slopes and a skyline of fells. Now turn left to follow the path up the broad ridge to the bare summit.

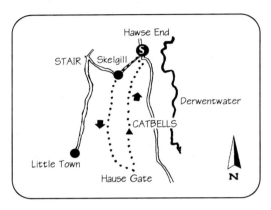

To west and east both of Catbells' flanks fall steeply from the summit, offering superlative presentations, respectively, of the uninterrupted two and a half thousand feet of the Grasmoor fells; and the royal blue of Derwentwater with its wooded islands and bays happily failing to conform to the normal finger-like pattern of the lakes. To the north mighty Skiddaw extends its broad shoulders, with Blencathra further right. Southwards, rugged fells are on display both down Borrowdale and at the head of Newlands. Foraging sheep having to nudge between reposing bodies are a reminder this exposed little summit is no place for the seeker of solitude.

Also revealed from the summit is the walk's return route along the north ridge. To return to the valley then, continue north along the ridge, on a worn path that descends enthusiastically over countless intervening outcrops, enjoying views over the lake and the Vale of Keswick that almost defy description. All too soon the foot of the ridge is neared, and the re-routed path zigzags down to the right to help alleviate erosion, curving left again just above the road junction. A level path runs straight on to the upper car park, otherwise drop right on a rebuilt path to the cattle-grid.

Looking west from Catbells: Ard Crags and Rigg Beck are overtopped by Wandope, Eel Crag, Sail and Scar Crags

```
┌─────────────────────────────────────┐
│              SUMMITS                 │
│  CAUSEY PIKE    2090ft/637m          │
│  SCAR CRAGS     2205ft/672m          │
└─────────────────────────────────────┘
```

START Stair   **Grid ref.** NY 231217

DISTANCE 4½ miles/7km   **ASCENT** 1935ft/590m

ORDNANCE SURVEY MAPS
1:50,000 - Landranger 89 **or** 90   1:25,000 - Outdoor Leisure 4

ACCESS Start from the Braithwaite-Buttermere road, just north of Stoneycroft. There is a roadside lay-by above Uzzicar. Braithwaite is served by Keswick-Cockermouth buses.

The grandest sight from the streets of Keswick is the Grasmoor group of fells, and the familiar outline that pushes itself to prominence is Causey Pike. This walk offers a direct, uncomplicated and quite superb climb to an airy summit.

S From the parking area head south along the road, above the house at Stoneycroft to Stonycroft Bridge. Looking up the lively beck, our main goal of Causey Pike throws down an irresistible challenge. Just 20 yards further a path leaves the road to commence the climb. Several level green ways are crossed before the path makes an early fork. To those with eyes focused on Causey Pike's summit, it is possible to miss the left branch, and certainly the right branch provides a gentler, more direct means of gaining the ridge. However, the main route onto Causey Pike's kid brother Rowling End is firmly recommended, for it divides the climb into two distinct sections and provides far superior early views.

Having branched left the steep climb continues, winding through heather for a steep but enjoyable assault of the nose end, with a short clamber over tilted rock before the going eases. Rowling End is not a true summit, merely the abrupt terminus of a ridge, but it is a classic point to reach. The unfolding views of the climb can now be savoured at leisure, looking back over the green fields of the Newlands Valley to Derwentwater, Keswick, Skiddaw and Blencathra. Catbells rises directly opposite, with the High Stile ridge appearing over Newlands Hause.

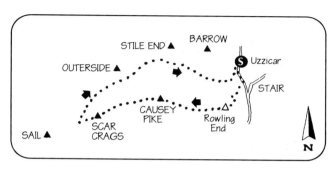

A further reward is a level few minutes on the path through the heather, meeting the direct path at a cairn at Sleet Hause, the base of the upper section of the climb. By now Bassenthwaite Lake has also appeared over Barrow Door. The well worn path sets to this final section with vigour, and as the going steepens a rock band awaits at the top. This very mild scramble offers an exhilarating means of gaining the summit. A scrappy cairn occupies the top, and the work is done. One can now fully appreciate Causey Pike's position as the abrupt, high level terminus of a much greater ridge, which rises in graded stages to the parent fell of Eel Crag. As the sandwiches emerge, eyes will share this mountain line-up with the splendid contrast of the Newlands and Derwentwater scene.

Resume along the broad path on the switchback ridge towards Scar Crags, enjoying a succession of identical knobbles. Beyond them the path drops to a more pronounced saddle. Scar Crags' southern flank now rears its head impressively, a striking line of shattered crags plunging towards Rigg Beck. Part way down this seemingly arid desert a stand of sessile oaks struggle gamely on, reputedly the highest surviving in the country. There is also a contrasting view across the grassy northern slopes to Force Crag and the old mine at the head of Coledale, far below the noble peak of Grisedale Pike. A gentle climb leads to the cairn which stands at the near end of a broader summit ridge.

*Rowling End
and
Causey Pike
from Skelgill,
below Catbells*

At the far end of the summit ridge the path drops within minutes to Sail Pass, its very distinct crossroads being the turning point of the walk. Unimpressed with the jaw-sagging prospect of the scarred path onto the bulk of Sail, ahead, double back to the right on a good path. This soon slants impressively down beneath the rough flank, with crags and heather above and scree below. The descent eases out after passing an old cobalt mine to reach the saddle of High Moss as a super path.

The broadening path is the former mine road that served the workings, and it now leads unfailingly down Stonycroft Gill, all the way back to the start. Just sit back and enjoy the journey. Note however that if keen for more tops, then from High Moss one might incorporate the Outerside-Barrow ridge, on the left. It is almost effortless and is described in WALK 14.

*Causey Pike
from Stair*

```
┌─────────────────────────────────────┐
│              SUMMITS                 │
│   OUTERSIDE    1863ft/568m           │
│   STILE END    1466ft/447m           │
│   BARROW       1492ft/455m           │
└─────────────────────────────────────┘
```

START Stair   **Grid ref.** NY 232217

DISTANCE 5 miles/8km   **ASCENT** 1805ft/550m

ORDNANCE SURVEY MAPS
1:50,000 - Landranger 89 **or** 90   1:25,000 - Outdoor Leisure 4

ACCESS Start from the Braithwaite-Buttermere road a mile south of Braithwaite. Shortly after the road opens out after a cattle-grid there is ample roadside parking by an old landslip, above the farm drive to Uzzicar. Braithwaite is served by Keswick-Cockermouth buses.

Extremely easy ascent work on a walk on lower fells in the very heart of higher peaks: richly contrasting scenery.

S The starting point is the site of the former Barrow Mine. Head south along the road, and a green bridlepath branches gently right 200 yards south of the Uzzicar drive. Precious little height is gained above Stoneycroft on this route which was skilfully constructed to serve a cobalt mine high in the heart of the mountains. At once there are outstanding views across Newlands to Catbells, with Walla Crag backed by Clough Head beyond.

Above Stonycroft Bridge the mine road turns to leave the Newlands Valley in order to make progress up the side valley of Stonycroft Gill. Over to the left Causey Pike makes first-class viewing while moving steadily up Barrow's colourful flanks, while up ahead is Outerside, highest peak of the walk. Simply stride out up the easy gradients of the mine road. A little beyond the last tree in the gill, with the flank of Barrow by now receded to a tame heather slope, a cairn indicates the point to leave the mine road if wanting to omit Outerside and Stile nd: a slim path doubles back to the right, gravitating marginally uphill to the heather defile of Barrow Door to where the main route will return.

The mine road meanwhile curves up to the left under Outerside's cone, to rise towards the environs of High Moss. After passing a sheepfold just below the track, slant right up the receding heather of Outerside's upper slopes to gain a nice path climbing from High Moss. Double back for the briefest of climbs, enjoying views down into Coledale, with its old mine buildings prominent beneath Force Crag.

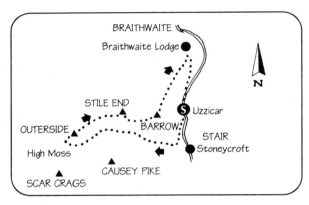

Outerside's summit is quickly gained, an unfashionable top that makes an unrivalled platform for appraising the lofty peaks rimming Coledale. Asserting its full stature directly opposite is the imposing specimen of Grisedale Pike, which appears far greater than its extra few hundred feet show. The austerity of the nearby mountain picture - in which Causey Pike for once appears much less recognisable - is offset by the offering from the other direction, where Derwentwater adds it regal charms beyond the verdant pastures of the Newlands Valley.

From the cairn a path descends the well defined ridge to the north-east, savouring the glorious all-round views. On gaining Low Moss ignore any branches and keep straight on past some small pools. A grassy path rises onto Stile End, passing just south of the summit. A tiny cairn sits on top, and strolling a few yards north earns a bird's-eye view of Braithwaite.

To reach Barrow Door just beneath it, turn back to the right on a thin path. This curves down to the well defined saddle, where paths snake purposely through robust heather. The most popular one heads straight up the broad ridge opposite onto Barrow's summit. A feeble cairn does scant justice to a prize-winning viewpoint, in which the horseshoe of Coledale's fells hover moodily above, the four tops of the Eel Crag ridge displayed individually from this flattering angle. The single jarring note is the concrete bridge spanning the Greta behind Keswick: not in a hundred years will it blend in. Sanity is restored by Derwentwater in the resplendent Vale of Keswick, a scene of exquisite loveliness made special by the profusion of trees.

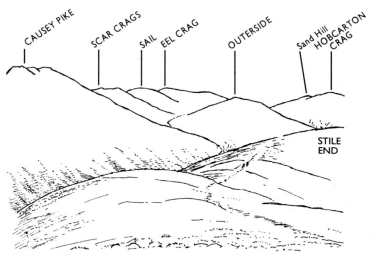

Looking west from Barrow, across Stonycroft Gill

There is one royal road down, this being the declining north ridge pointing towards the white walls and grey roofs of Braithwaite. First through heather and then bracken, every step is absolute joy. Near the foot of the ridge above Braithwaite Lodge farm, a wide green cross-roads is reached. The right branch doubles back above a plantation to reluctantly rejoin the road along Barrow's base, enjoying a classic finale overlooking the Newlands scene. The starting point is only a little farther along the broad verged road.

SUMMITS
GRISEDALE PIKE   2595ft/791m
HOBCARTON CRAG   2425ft/739m

START Braithwaite   **Grid ref.** NY 230236

DISTANCE 7½ miles/12km   **ASCENT** 2460ft/750m

ORDNANCE SURVEY MAPS
1:50,000 - Landranger 89 **or** 90   1:25,000 - Outdoor Leisure 4

ACCESS Start from the village centre. There are numerous careful parking places, and a small car park on the Whinlatter road (en route) above the village. Braithwaite is served by Keswick-Cockermouth buses and seasonal Keswick-Buttermere buses.

Grisedale Pike projects itself assertively above Coledale, its elegant outline encapsulated in a classic profile when seen across the broad sweep of Derwentwater. This walk tackles its tiered east ridge, a splendid, uncomplicated route to a fine summit.

❺ Braithwaite is departed by the road heading for Whinlatter Pass, and this in turn is left at a parking area on the left. A narrow path climbs to its right, soon merging into a much broader one before rising through bracken onto the broad green ridge of Kinn. The steep pull is relieved by retrospective views over the grey and white houses of Braithwaite to the Vale of Keswick, backed by the mass of the Skiddaw group.

The entire walk is now in prospect, with an impressive array of peaks hemming in the deep valley of Coledale. The immediate task is the pleasurable one of attaining the top of Grisedale Pike, which shines like a beacon ahead. After a few more hundred feet the heathery crest of Sleet How is gained, and the finest section of this east ridge draws the eager walker up through a slaty stairway that invites modest scrambles for a fitting conclusion to the ascent.

Grisedale Pike's bare top offers one of Lakeland's finer views, its special appeal being variety. To the south-east is a skyline in which the great peaks contest elbow room, while a contrast is formed by a combination of the Derwentwater scene on one side and the drama of Hobcarton Crag beneath the neat peak of Hopegill Head on the other.

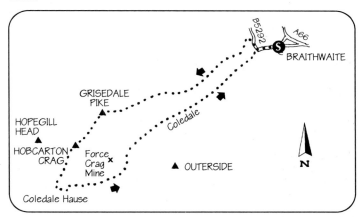

From this airy, windswept crown a well blazed path heads south-west along the slaty ridge, soon halting its decline when faced by the subsidiary top of Hobcarton Crag. A short pull gains this intervening top, and within a hundred yards of resuming the descent a major fork is reached. The main route takes the left arm, which sets a direct course for Coledale Hause: it drops steadily past old mineshafts to gain the grassy saddle. Across this broad pass (which is seldom used as such) loom the bulky pair of Eel Crag and Grasmoor. *For an enjoyable diversion, the inviting right branch clings to the rim of the Hobcarton valley to climb above Hobcarton Crag proper to gain the slender summit of Hopegill Head. To rejoin the main route, a broad path heads south-east over the top of Sand Hill before dropping to Coledale Hause.*

The Grisedale Pike and Hopegill Head paths meet on the true crest of Coledale Hause. Advance 100 yards further to a fork, where both arms rise steadily away. The left branch quickly leads to the broad course of the path climbing out of the head of Coledale. Turn left down it to reveal the dead-straight return course of Coledale pointing towards

Skiddaw and Blencathra, while Eel Crag frowns darkly above us. The well worn path winds fairly steeply down into the upper basin of Pudding Beck, a fine example of a hanging valley. Over to the left are some mining remains beneath the falls of High Force spouting over the vegetated crag.

Escaping this hollow the path winds down, for a rough half-mile underfoot as Force Crag is revealed to the left. Here the upper scene is replicated on a much grander scale, now with Low Force spilling over a similarly vegetated crag. Below are the decaying buildings of the old Force Crag Mine, which was still operating in the early 1990s. Though in truth nothing more than an eyesore, there is an endearing familiarity about these rotting remains that makes them an integral part of the scene.

The old track improves underfoot and slants down the fell to cross Coledale Beck and rise to the old mine road. This is followed away for an exceptionally easy conclusion. If returning to the Whinlatter road car park, remain on the mine road which terminates there. Nearing Braithwaite, however, look out for a branch path on the right immediately after a kink in the track. The path runs a parallel course below, before dropping down onto the Whinlatter road on the edge of the village.

Grisedale Pike from Hobcarton Crag,
with Skiddaw and Blencathra behind

> **SUMMITS**
> BARF   1536ft/468m
> LORD'S SEAT   1811ft/552m

START *Beckstones*   **Grid ref.** *NY 220264*

DISTANCE *5 miles/8km*   **ASCENT** *1700ft/518m*

ORDNANCE SURVEY MAPS
*1:50,000 - Landranger 89 **or** 90*   *1:25,000 - Outdoor Leisure 4*

ACCESS *Start from the National Park car park at Powter How, north of the Swan Hotel (1 mile north of Thornthwaite off the A66). Served by Keswick-Cockermouth buses.*

Undisputed overlord of the fells north of Whinlatter Pass, Lord's Seat offers nothing spectacular other than being a pleasant height to which to aspire, though the inclusion of Barf adds a livelier element.

S   From the green outside the *Swan Hotel* a narrow road sets off through the trees across the former main road. It crosses Beckstones Gill to the house at Beckstones, but once over the bridge it can be vacated at a stile on the right. A good path climbs by the beck to eventually submerge itself in the trees of Beckstones Plantation. During the lower part of the climb there are ample opportunities to appraise the wild face of Barf across the beck, and in particular to locate its whitewashed Bishop.

This famous cleric is a long established landmark in these parts, and a less civilised route from the roadside trees could be engaged to incorporate his slaty self, but only for those prepared for an ungainly scramble. The presence of slate all around makes his exposed pulpit even more precarious, for the outcropping rocks, including those from which he preaches, are friable in the extreme. He is, however, of such importance that he regularly receives a new coat from a zealous decorator from down below.

Back in the plantation, height is gained with less difficulty, though initially very steeply. Glimpses of the heathery flanks of Barf show its aggressiveness to be rapidly receding. Excitement is provided by a minor scramble up a band of rock across the path. On meeting a broad green forest way, turn right along it: this swings uphill to remain within the plantation, but almost at once vacate it by making for a prominent stile in the fence. Suddenly outside the trees, a charming path re-crosses Beckstones Gill and makes its way happily up gentle slopes to Barf's grassy top.

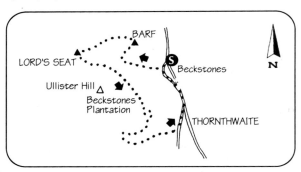

A scrappy cairn on a tame knoll contrasts sharply with the dubious thrills and spills of the aforementioned direct ascent, but this is a smashing point to reach, having saved the splendid bird's-eye view of Bassenthwaite Lake for a finale. Barf's awesome appearance above the *Swan Hotel* is further enhanced by the fact that its tumble of crag, scree, heather and gorse is the only patch of fellside for some miles above Bassenthwaite Lake untamed by the foresters.

After consuming the majestic prospect of the Skiddaw group rising beyond the vast waters of Bassenthwaite, steps can turn to the undemanding slopes in the opposite direction, where the grassy dome of Lord's Seat beckons. An obvious path heads off, making directly for the intervening depression before a climb that involves an unexpected disappointingly boggy tract before the final pull. Two forlorn straining posts occupy the windy top, though one may be collapsed. This hierarch of the Whinlatter fells offers views appropriate to its status. These include a good side-on picture of the Skiddaw group beyond Barf, a glimpse into the lonely Aiken valley to the south-west, and a typically first-class pose by Grisedale Pike, across Whinlatter.

The route of departure is south, towards the extensive plantations that together form Whinlatter Forest. The forest fence runs only a short distance below the summit dome, and the main path descends to the right-hand of two stiles. From it a built path heads away, and like it or not one must concede it makes light work of the marshy terrain. Running casually through the heather in the direction of the tree-free Ullister Hill ahead, there is clearly no haste to plunge into the forest proper. At two junctions our chosen route bears left each time, passing curious pockets of conifers before turning more sharply left to descend more markedly: ahead, the ascent over Barf is well seen. The path drop down to the inevitable, the terminus of a forest road. Follow this along to the right, numbers in brackets from here-on relate to forest marker posts, which make useful guides.

So begins a prolonged descent through Beckstones Plantation, the upper half of which accompanies forest roads that decline ever cautiously to facilitate the passage of vehicles. This first section is followed gently down for about three-quarters of a mile, and long after passing two lesser roads doubling back to the left (7 & 8), a wide junction (9) is reached. With a gap in the trees permitting a fine prospect of Causey Pike straight ahead, turn left to double back down a hairpin bend, and down to another junction (11) where this time the northern ridges of Grisedale Pike are neatly revealed. Only a handful of yards along to the right, an innocuous green path slopes off from this abnormally wide road, a little gem that slants down to become a track and crosses Comb Gill. Immediately over, take a waymarked path on the left, soon re-crossing and shadowing the colourful stream down to an old sheepfold.

Below the fold re-cross to join another path, resuming downstream to quickly reach a bigger path junction. Here go left, crossing Comb Gill one last time before slanting down to meet a forest road. This is happily crossed straight over to make acquaintance with tumbling Comb Beck. In idyllic surroundings, like woodland was meant to be, it is shadowed downstream, passing an old mine level. A gate leads out of the woods, where a novel entry onto a narrow lane leads past white houses to emerge onto a back road in Thornthwaite. Turning left and keeping left, the road runs above the village to join the main road through it. The *Swan Hotel* is now only minutes further, and this already quiet road can be left by a road to the left after the last house to finish by way of the start, at Beckstones. A prize feature of the concluding half-mile is a fine prospect of Barf.

SUMMITS
SALE FELL   1178ft/359m

START Wythop   **Grid ref.** NY 199306

DISTANCE 4 miles/6½km   **ASCENT** 1000ft/305m

ORDNANCE SURVEY MAPS
1:50,000 - Landranger 89 **or** 90   1:25,000 - Outdoor Leisure 4

ACCESS Start from the Pheasant Inn. Parking on the wide road nearby, bypassed by the modern A66. Served by Keswick-Cockermouth buses.

Sale Fell sits on the edge of true fell country, and its dry, springy turf is an absolute joy to walk upon, allied to which are some fine views over Bassenthwaite Lake to the Skiddaw massif.

S From the junction by the inn take the road signposted to Wythop Mill, rising steadily past several dwellings. Approaching the brow, take a kissing-gate on the left, from where Wythop Church appears just along the road. From the gate a broad green path slants up to a similar gate onto the open fell. Views over the church feature the Vale of Embleton, while looking back the foot of Bassenthwaite Lake can be seen. Just above the gate is a terrace path, which is followed right. In springtime the bank below is delightfully coloured by hawthorn and gorse.

The path slants up to meet a wall, and with neighbouring Ling Fell appearing ahead, together they rise to the brow on Sale Fell's west ridge. Forsake the main path for a slender one breasting the grassy ridge. This quickly forks, the right branch being nicer as it curves up to take in the crest of the rock garden of Dodd Crag above the secluded Wythop Valley. Keeping to the height of land the other faint branch is regained, passing a small quarry site to attain the noteworthy summit cairn.

The next objective is the grassy shelf of Lothwaite, in the direction of Skiddaw to the east. Incomparably easy walking resumes as the path runs down the slope, through a gate in a rebuilt wall. Through a collapsed wall just beyond, bear left below a cairned top to a little col: here a thinner path takes up the running to rise left onto Lothwaite's highest point at 1132ft/345m. The already memorable view of Skiddaw and its ridges is now surpassed with the addition of Bassenthwaite Lake to provide full depth of foreground: this prospect is quite the highlight of the walk.

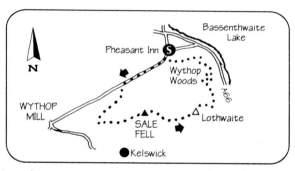

Continue the remaining way along the ridge to the edge of Wythop Woods, and a short descent to the right will meet a broad green path entering the trees. Within a matter of yards it meets the hairpin of a forest road, and a typically dawdling descent now ensues. The first stage enjoys the delights of a lovely beechwood on the steep slopes to the right. Remaining on the main track it zigzags down through several junctions, taking the downhill branch at each turn. At a particularly major junction a splendid open prospect over the lake to Skiddaw greets the eye, and turning down to the left the administrative centre of Thornthwaite Forest is seen just below.

There are several ways to finish. From the centre a surfaced drive leads out to the road on which the walk began, but as there can be vehicles and machinery on the move, a nicer finish leaves the track above it, running along to the left. This leads out to the road higher up, but better still, join the centre's drive part-way on and double back a short way to a minor dip. Here take a faint grassy way doubling back down to the left, becoming clearer as it levels out at a gate. It runs inside the edge of the wood to emerge onto the lawn of the *Pheasant Inn*.

SUMMITS	
ULLOCK PIKE	2270ft/692m
LONG SIDE	2408ft/734m
CARL SIDE	2447ft/746m
SKIDDAW	3054ft/931m
BAKESTALL	2208ft/673m

START High Side   **Grid ref.** NY 236309

DISTANCE 9 miles/14½km   **ASCENT** 2900ft/884m

ORDNANCE SURVEY MAPS
1:50,000 - Landranger 89 **or** 90   1:25,000 - Outdoor Leisure 4

ACCESS Start from a prominent parking area along the minor road to Orthwaite, just a quarter-mile off the A591 at High Side. The main road is served by Keswick-Carlisle buses.

The multi-topped ridge of Longside Edge is the connoisseur's route onto Skiddaw, making a superb horseshoe of seldom frequented Southerndale.

⑤ Just yards beyond the lay-by, towards Barkbeth, a gate on the right sees a grassy bridlepath slant up to the left. Beyond a tiny stream this old drove road is deflected uphill by a line of hawthorns. Ahead, already, the dark heights of Skiddaw and the enticing crest of Ullock Pike await, while Bassenthwaite Lake occupies a deep trench below. The track doubles back and crosses another pasture before swinging up to gain the open fell above Southerndale Beck, a grand moment.

The track into this valley haven is at once vacated to gain an immediate foothold on the ridge up to the right, a veritable stairway to heaven. First feature of note is the cluster of Watches, a curious arrangement of boulders on a saddle. Beyond this briefly level section a thin path quickly becomes clearer as the slopes gain both height and form amid the heather and bilberry of the knobbly ridge known as The

Edge. Sweeping views over glistening Bassenthwaite Lake contrast with the massive grey bulk of Skiddaw as steps are drawn to the beckoning peak of Ullock Pike.

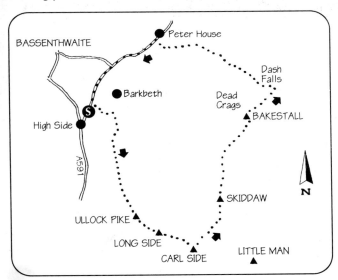

Although set back a few yards from the cone that drew us, the summit cannot fail to impress. From this windswept perch the eastern flank rolls majestically down to Southerndale backed by the powerful mass of Skiddaw, while the other side reveals Bassenthwaite Lake in unparalleled splendour. Whilst savouring its view, note the appearance of the Coniston tops far beyond the lower central fells: the fact that these mountains sit at the opposite end of the Lake District only serves to emphasise the compactness of this region. Closer to hand, the Coledale Fells, marshalled by the striking Grisedale Pike, acquit themselves to their usual standards. Only on touching the cairn is Derwentwater revealed in its entirety, with a full backing of the Borrowdale fells.

Back on the ridge, meanwhile, it is bit a few short minutes onto the greater top of Long Side, though it is unfortunate it could not have exerted itself another 50 or so feet and thus gained the superiority it deserves over neighbouring Carl Side. Its cairn perches on a luxuriant couch above an exceedingly steep drop into Southerndale. The short while it takes to link these tops along Longside Edge provide first-class fellwalking: savour the moment! Long Side's virtues as a viewpoint are plentiful, for away from the permanent gaze of Skiddaw there is a wonderful panorama of every type of country, from the Solway Firth and the many miles of coastline inland to Bassenthwaite Lake at our feet, Ullock Pike and Southerndale even nearer, and a host of mountain tops ranged across the centre of the district.

Resuming, the path skirts the Southerndale rim to the Carl Side col, occupied by the tiny pool of Carlside Tarn. Collectors of summits will however first strike out to take in the rounded top of Carl Side. This is the highest but least interesting of the three tops occupying the ascent ridge. Its advantage over Long Side and Ullock Pike is that it boasts a south-facing front, and the view from the cairn in its sea of grass can be improved by wandering a little further to the south. Here a better foreground is given to the magnificent mountain prospect to the south and west of Derwentwater. Another ascent path is met at the cairn, which leads back to the merging of paths by the tarn.

Here the final stage of the ascent presents itself, as a path slants obliquely across the scree-draped upper flank of Skiddaw. Looking back down, the earlier ascent ridge appears well dwarfed. Although this upper section steepens towards the top, the good path makes relatively light work of things to suddenly ease at a shelter on the airy summit ridge. A two-minute saunter to the left along the broad, high level ridge leads quickly to the popular summit of Skiddaw, lowest member of Lakeland's exclusive '3000' club. The highest point is crowned by an Ordnance Survey column adrift in a sea of erosion, while a view indicator, cairns and numerous shelters litter the top. The underlying rock here is Skiddaw slate, which reputedly makes Skiddaw the district's oldest mountain.

While one obviously expects to feel uplifted at this altitude, there is a particularly keen awareness of this on Skiddaw's exposed top, due to the mountain's isolation from similarly high ground. In contrast, the other 3000-footers are supported by lofty colleagues. Such isolation guarantees an excellent picture of Lakeland's various mountain groups to the south. Other aspects of the view vary from the belt of trees sheltering lonely Skiddaw House deep in the bowl of Skiddaw Forest, to an extensive coastline from the Solway Firth out to the Irish Sea, across which the Galloway Hills and the Isle of Man can look very close on clear days.

Having flirted with the crowds, resume by continuing north past two more shelters, with the route over Broad End and Bakestall appearing below. The descent proper begins by passing above Gibraltar Crag on the left before dropping onto a plateau. Here the path fades, and in poor visibility a couple of cairns point the way to a fence on the right. A path reforms and descends with the fence to Bakestall. An old sheepfold occupies a minor col as the tiniest of rises leads to a cairn at the fence corner. From here a path runs 100 yards out to a lower cairn for a splendid view over the Dash Valley and out to Overwater.

The flanks of mighty Skiddaw offer little in the way of cliffs, but at 2000 feet on these northern slopes there commences a spectacular plunge known as Dead Crags: it is thanks to this feature that Skiddaw's satellite Bakestall earns modest recognition. With no sign of Dead Crags yet, contour right to rejoin path and fence, or seek out a trod which forms above the appearing crags. A great moment occurs as the true edge of the crags is gained just yards short of the fence, revealing a wall of crag and scree on a scale not expected. An easy descent of Birkett Edge drops onto the rough road serving Skiddaw House, once a shepherd's bothy and now an exceedingly remote youth hostel.

Turning left the road winds down beneath Dead Crags, and only on levelling out are the effervescent Dash Falls revealed back to the right. The surfaced road from Dash Farm is joined to lead out through lush pastures to the Orthwaite road at Peter House. Turn left to conclude. Virtually traffic-free, with leafy hedgerows and increasingly good views over the day's fells, this makes a pleasing conclusion. On nearing the end, Bassenthwaite village is well seen amongst a neatly parcelled and quintessential English landscape.

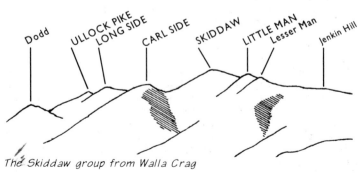

The Skiddaw group from Walla Crag

> **SUMMITS**
> GREAT COCKUP   1726ft/526m
> MEAL FELL   1804ft/550m

START Orthwaite   **Grid ref.** NY 252340

DISTANCE 5½ miles/9km   **ASCENT** 1365ft/416m

ORDNANCE SURVEY MAPS
1:50,000 - Landranger 89 **or** 90   1:25,000 - Outdoor Leisure 4

ACCESS Start from the hamlet of Orthwaite on a minor road north-east of Bassenthwaite village. Parking is limited to several verges between Orthwaite and Horsemoor Hills farm: take care not to block access, in particular the drive where the walk begins. Bassenthwaite (2 miles) is served by bus from Keswick, Workington and Carlisle.

An undemanding ramble in the relaxing country 'back o'Skidda'.

S On the road descending from Orthwaite to Horsemoor Hills, a bridleway sign signals the start of the walk, along a farm drive on the left. Outstanding views rapidly unfold over the Dash Valley to the seldom seen northern flanks of Skiddaw: the group is ranged magnificently from Bakestall to Ullock Pike. Bassenthwaite Lake adds early variety across to the right.

On rounding a corner the foaming tumble of Dash Falls (also known as Whitewater Dash) is revealed at the valley head, with the Skiddaw House road climbing above it. Just past this corner the level track is vacated in favour of a signposted green path that slants up to the left through bracken. It climbs effortlessly to fade at a minor col behind a tiny outcrop, a place to halt and savour the surroundings. Resuming, the way quickly re-establishes itself for a very gradual rise along the flank of Great Cockup's ridge. Through the gap above Dash Falls, Lonscale Fell's east peak puts in a sudden, dramatic appearance.

At its highest point the green way can be vacated for a broad grassy break in the heather, which rises direct onto the broad ridgetop. The crest is gained at a sunken, circular shooting butt. The newly revealed views north look over the villages of the Cumberland Plain to a vast sweep of the Solway Firth, backed by the Dumfries-shire landmark of Criffel. Turn right on a faint trod which scales the final slope past a line of abandoned butts, fading as it points the way to a prominent cairn.

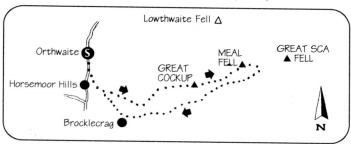

Standing on the western end of the vast summit plateau, this is a superior viewpoint to the summit. Features of note include the shy tarn of Overwater to the north. In good visibility Criffel can seem almost within a stone's throw, and might be backed by the Galloway Hills to its left and the Moffat Hills to its right. Out to sea, the distinguished Snaefell marks the highest point of the Isle of Man. While some of these features are visible from many a northern or western Lakeland fell, they demand more attention from the likes of Great Cockup which has a less than stunning picture of its own hills.

The true summit cairn now waits just across the pathless grassy crest to the east. With the modern translation of 'enormous blunder' to its name, Great Cockup may be the object of some mirth, but is rarely the object of a fellwalk. It is the westernmost of the Uldale Fells, linked tenuously to its parent fell of Knott by way of the adjacent Meal Fell and Great Sca Fell. Having surveyed the distant panorama, one's eyes are readily drawn to a less obstructed picture of the Skiddaw massif, fronted in style by the dark shadow of Dead Crags under Bakestall.

Bizarrely, the next objective of Meal Fell might be difficult to locate, for though higher, it is rendered anonymous by the loftier heights of the Great and Little Sca Fells behind it. From the top then, continue along the ridge. A thin path forms on a gentle, grassy descent. Suddenly the otherwise innocuous slope falls away into the broken wall of Trusmadoor, the atmospheric little pass linking with Meal Fell, where rough scree slopes brood over a narrow divide. On its craggy lip turn down to the right to the small cairn marking the head of this novel defile in these otherwise docile hills.

Only yards down to the right is Burntod Gill, and if wishing to omit Meal Fell, simply join the stream. For Meal Fell take the path climbing away from the cairn, but after the initial steepness strike off up the pathless slopes (much less daunting than they appeared from across Trusmadoor). Before long the going will ease and the surprisingly interesting summit will be underfoot. It is possible that Meal Fell is the smallest in Lakeland when one surveys its well defined boundaries, yet even these insignificant acres provide features of note. A large pile of stones, fashioned into a circular shelter, stands on a mound, while a comparatively lonely cairn stands across a puddle-strewn depression. A scattering of stones in the vicinity further adds to the scene.

Unless wishing to retrace steps to Trusmadoor, commence the return by advancing further along the ridge, on a thin trod making for Great Sca Fell. Within two minutes the saddle is reached, and here turn down to the right to drop into the level floor of the miniature ravine of Frozenfell Gill. Although one could remain on higher level sheeptrods, a thoroughly enjoyable walk clings to the tiny beck, an utterly enchanting interlude. In these deep walled environs the stream is recrossed countless times to return to the slope under Trusmadoor.

The continuing Burntod Gill offers a similar option for the next, slightly less intimate stage. One could also rise up a few feet again to trace a clear, contouring trod that generally keeps above the screes falling to the gill. Suddenly the gill opens out into a larger valley, and after a last look back at Meal Fell head away past a crumbling sheep bield (shelter). Cross the pathless slope behind it to merge into a broad green path rising from the beck - this is the bridleway on which the walk began. This gently scales the bracken flank, and if retained will lead all the way back, picking up the outward route on the brow.

Soon after joining the bridleway a level trod forks left. It briefly enters a marshy section before contouring along to the intake wall. Running above it, this path also makes an enjoyable return, maintaining its height when the wall drops away, to run more faintly on to the base of the tumble of quartz-streaked boulders of Brockle Crag. A little further it drops to join the drive above the farmhouse at Brocklecrag, whose central grass strip makes a splendid conclusion to the walk.

SUMMITS
BANNERDALE CRAGS 2241ft/683m
BOWSCALE FELL 2303ft/702m

START Mungrisdale   **Grid ref.** NY 362302

DISTANCE 5½ miles/9km   **ASCENT** 1720ft/524m

ORDNANCE SURVEY MAPS
1:50,000 - Landranger 90   1:25,000 - Outdoor Leisure 5

ACCESS Start from the village centre. There is a roadside parking area opposite the village hall, below the Mill Inn (honesty box for parking fees). There are seasonal buses from Keswick and Carlisle.

Only from Mungrisdale does Bannerdale Crags reveal its true self, a tantalising glimpse to attract the discerning: neatly portrayed is the splendid east face. The meandering Glenderamackin provides the perfect guide into a quiet bowl among the hills, from where a broad green ridge transforms into a spectacular arete leading directly to the summit.

S Leave the village at the hairpin bend between pub and church, on a rough lane setting off from the telephone box. The lane is short-lived, and through a gate open country is entered on an inviting track in the company of the river Glenderamackin. Ahead is the rounded cone of the Tongue, with Bannerdale Crags set further back to the left. After crossing inflowing Bullfell Beck the main track rises away from the river, but a thinner path branches left to remain true to it. Note that the track offers easy access to the ridge linking the walk's two summits.

Initially rather enclosed, the riverside path opens out to see Bannerdale Crags now directly ahead, sending a green tongue down for us (illustrated on page 1). After crossing Bannerdale Beck by the remains of a sheepfold, forsake the tempting green path by the river, and zigzag up the bank. This lesser path now rises through bracken to a

along the improving grassy ridge to the base of
s' east ridge proper. This impressive arete has loomed
time, and at last it can be scaled.

n commences the ascent, weaving between haphazard
.te. The remains of a stone hut survive from old lead mining
ope. .ns, and still offer some form of shelter. Above it some modest
scrambling options begin, but given the unreliable nature of slate
there is little shame in avoiding the direct route by keeping to a grassier
path on the left. The delights of this face are further enhanced by a
colourful fusion of heather and bilberry on the steep slopes to the right.

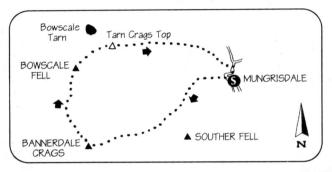

At the top of the outcrops the going suddenly eases, and a short grassy
rise leads to a cairn just above the edge. By this stage Blencathra has
revealed itself ahead, with its alternative name of Saddleback needing
little explanation; the spiky ridge of Sharp Edge rises to the right-hand
peak of Foule Crag. A short 100 yards west across the top Bannerdale
Crags' summit cairn awaits, on featureless grass. This unsung stalwart
receives scant mention in fellwalking circles, despite its arresting face
being especially noteworthy in these predominantly grassy northern-
most fells. The view now embraces the emptiness of Skiddaw Forest,
with Skiddaw itself and the Caldbeck Fells enclosing this lonely basin.

Resume by returning to the edge to pick up a continuing path, a grand
stroll around the head of Bannerdale. Ahead wait the gentle slopes of
Bowscale Fell, but look back also to be suitably impressed by that
ascent route. As the path turns beyond the crags to begin to descend,
a faint trod breaks off to cross moister ground to the base of Bowscale
Fell's upper slopes. A better path re-establishes itself for the modest
rise to the summit, where a shelter occupies the highest point.

Surveying the panorama, Blencathra is very much the dominan
mountain: from here it boasts several peaks, and a fertile imagination
might liken it to Torridon's Beinn Eighe. There are good sightings of
Pillar and High Stile and the shapely cones of Grisedale Pike and
Hopegill Head, while near at hand again, Skiddaw patrols the
wilderness of its 'forest'. Having picked out the fells, the chief focus
of attention might be outside of Lakeland, when a clear day reveals
such far-flung uplands as the Galloway Hills and the North Pennines,
all ranged beyond mile upon mile of neatly packaged farmland.

Bowscale Fell's special feature is yet to come, for its northern flank
shelters a jewel of a mountain tarn in a perfectly hollowed comb. To
find it resume by heading north-east past a cairn some 75 yards
beyond the shelter, a path quickly re-forming to drop to a minor saddle
before fading. Rise towards a cairned knoll, and veer a few yards left
to reveal the fine prospect of the elusive tarn in its glacial hollow. A
line of modest crags rim this delectable bowl, over which the well
sited subsidiary of Tarn Crags Top keeps a watchful eye. A short pull
to the right leads onto its twin-cairned top.

The return to Mungrisdale is a first-class march down the broad crest
of the east ridge, a feature of which is the presence of several splendid
cairns. With Carrock Fell to the left and Bannerdale Crags back to the
right, this is a splendid stride on a good path. The village is revealed
before a steeper drop through colourful vegetation. Only at the end
is real steeper ground encountered, so be sure to locate an inviting
grassy rake down to the right to avoid crags. Dropping through gorse
the path empties onto a track at the bottom corner of the fell, by an old
quarry. Go left through a gate and onto the road at the edge of the
village. Turning right to finish, a short-cut can be made at the bend
after the tiny church of St. Kentigern by taking a gate in front and then
along a fieldside back to the hall.

Blencathra from Bowscale Fell

77

CARROCK FELL

```
SUMMITS
CARROCK FELL    2175ft/663m
HIGH PIKE       2159ft/658m
```

START Mosedale   **Grid ref.** NY 356321

DISTANCE 7½ miles/12km   **ASCENT** 1785ft/544m

ORDNANCE SURVEY MAPS
1:50,000 - Landranger 90   1:25,000 - Outdoor Leisure 5

ACCESS *Start from the road junction by the telephone box. There is verge parking on the road by the two bridges south of the hamlet, or on the cul-de-sac road heading west through the hamlet. There are seasonal buses from Keswick and Carlisle.*

Two fells of differing but equally appealing character combine for this rewarding walk. Carrock Fell owes its ruggedness to the presence of volcanic rocks in an area where Skiddaw slate predominates. The outstanding geological arrangements provide further interest with a surround of defunct mine workings, while early man erected a stone fort on the very summit. High Pike is Lakeland's most northerly 2000-footer, and the overlord of the Caldbeck Fells. This vast tract of generally grassy terrain provides endless miles of easy walking, in surroundings that are a tonic for the jaded mind and the seeker of relative solitude.

S Depart Mosedale by the dead-end road to Swineside. Within a minute it becomes unenclosed, so make an immediate start to the climb by turning up a grassy path on the adjacent rough flank: this initial stage of the ascent is the only part of the route that could be described as strenuous, and this is soon forgotten amid the concentration needed to keep tabs on the path. Passing through gorse, heather and rashes of stones, the playful path can be faithfully followed with care, remembering that it never strays far from a direct line above the farmhouse on the road below. A well stamped section through a larger collection of stones is an obvious point to muster the troops, above which a grassier, easier way rises through heather to suddenly arrive at a three-sided bield (sheep shelter) perched near the edge.

Already the hard work is over. From here a grassy way maintains the north-westerly direction through the heather. On a brow just above, the upper reaches of the fell are revealed across a broad, heathery plateau bedecked with boulders. The super little path runs clearly on beneath a cairned knoll, soon rising again towards the summit. Bowscale Fell rises to the left across Mosedale, with the sprawling Knott beyond. The path eventually falters on more mixed terrain, but by now it is but a simple rise to the summit environs.

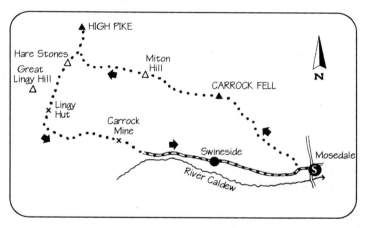

A fainter way resurrects itself for the final stage, gaining the top at a crumbling high-level sheepfold complex. The stones were no doubt recycled from the Iron Age hillfort that existed here, and its ribbon of stones is still very evident. Follow it left a short way to lead to the highest point, marked by a very well built cairn. Evidence of the ancient fortification abounds in the shape of crumbling walls, and the rich covering of vegetation makes this an altogether colourful and enjoyable place to be.

Carrock Fell is well placed to appraise Bowscale Fell's flank harbouring its secretive tarn in a hollowed comb rimmed by a line of modest crags; and to stare deep into the unfrequented bowl of Skiddaw Forest.

This situation on the very fringe of Lakeland also ensures a spacious prospect of the lowlands stretching away to the distant Pennines. This particular aspect is greatly enhanced by a walk out to the cairned East peak, whence the slopes fall rapidly to the pastures of Calebrack.

Two miles distant, High Pike is Carrock's nearest neighbour, and the way thereto is laid out in front. Prominent on its eastern flank is the former Driggith Mine, and the walk will pass through the heart of a mine later on. A path drops down through the old wall and heads west along the wide ridge, encountering marshy ground in the early stages as the knoll of Round Knott is passed. Approaching the subtle rise of Miton Hill, a cairn on a rash of stones signals the start of a magnificent grassy path, with High Pike's cairn beckoning throughout.

A modest saddle is reached at a crossroads with the Red Gate (an equally fine path), before a gentle pull onto the aptly named Drygill Head. Here the path forks, and the right arm swings round the head of the ravine to meet an old shooters' track. Crossing straight over, a path rises steadily and quickly to High Pike's summit, where first-time visitors will be astonished by its embellishments. Pride of place must go to a slate memorial seat, behind which is located an Ordnance Survey column and an immense, sprawling cairn and shelter.

A study of the view will largely be directed at the seemingly endless miles of farmland stretching into the haze of infinity, though in fairness the Scafell - and to a lesser degree, High Street - group slot in commendably between the bulky fells across Skiddaw Forest. A 50 yard stroll to the north cairn reveals a view of Caldbeck and its environs. It is to Caldbeck that High Pike gives allegiance, and to the people of the small fellside communities hereabouts it also offered employment in the scattering of mining operations on its flanks. Beyond the cairn is the well depleted ruin of a shepherd's hut.

Return to the shooters' track and follow it right (southerly), with the rounded top of Hare Stones just yards off to the right. Ahead, the rear view of Blencathra dominates things. The track descends more roughly and runs on beneath a set of sheep pens to end at the Lingy Hut. This former shooters' cabin is now put to good use as a shelter from the elements, and is maintained as a bothy by the National Park Authority. Beyond the hut a path takes up the reins for the stroll to Grainsgill Beck, which is charged with the task of draining Miller Moss.

Don't cross the stream but take a thinner path left, immediately commencing a descent of its bank. Though only thin its course remains clear. Ahead, Mosedale reaches back towards the hamlet, with Carrock Fell and Bowscale Fell framing it and the Carrock Mine site just below us. Part way down the path becomes fainter, and steps have been tempted left by a long drained water cut that once served the mine. This leads to another path dropping down to cross the stream of Arm o'Grain at some low ruins.

Both paths continue down the valley to reach the edge of the Carrock Mine site. It is important to remember that dangerous shafts lurk in wait for those who stray from the paths. A rough road quickly takes over, remaining near the beck to leave the mine and join the head of the cul-de-sac road from Mosedale. Looking back, the Lingy Hut stands silhouetted on the skyline.

To finish simply advance along the road, initially in the company of the substantial watercourse of the lovely river Caldew. Carrock Fell's flank also provides colourful company, with a jumble of bracken, gorse, scree, juniper and heather. With its grassy verges the road offers a gentle conclusion to this lonely walk 'back o' Skidda'. Observant eyes will see the curious Roundhouse in the trees by the first buildings.

Bowscale Fell and Blencathra from Miton Hill, Carrock Fell

SUMMITS
BLENCATHRA   2848ft/868m

START *Scales*   **Grid ref.** *NY 342268*

DISTANCE *4 miles/6½km*   **ASCENT** *2182ft/665m*

ORDNANCE SURVEY MAPS
1:50,000 - Landranger 90   1:25,000 - Outdoor Leisure 5

ACCESS Start from a roadside lay-by on the A66 to the west of the hamlet, just past Toll Bar Cottage at Scales Green. There is limited parking in Scales itself, near the White Horse Inn. Served by Penrith-Keswick buses and seasonal Keswick-Patterdale and Keswick-Mungrisdale services.

Of Blencathra's many ridges Sharp Edge offers the greatest challenge, an exhilarating scramble above a dramatically sited glacial tarn. There is also a soft option for those overtaken by nerves or high winds.

S The base of the fell is gained at a public footpath sign by Toll Bar Cottage. From a kissing-gate the main path slants right, up through bracken and leaving the intake wall behind to rise above the Mousthwaite Comb. It contours around the base of Scales Fell, above rougher ground to a point just above Mousthwaite Col. On rounding a corner the next stage of the path can be seen contouring ahead, as one of the most spectacular sights in Lakeland greets the eye.

This is Foule Crag, its flat top breaking into a sheer drop to the spiky ridge of Sharp Edge. After a good stride the path swings left to climb by Scales Beck (take care on rocks) to the edge of Scales Tarn. This sombre hollow (legend has it that the tarn is bottomless) is a place of great atmosphere. Be aware that Sharp Edge sees accidents in summer as well as winter: if high winds or ice, or a general unease in exposed places dictate that the edge be omitted, then a soft option is the clear path re-crossing the outflow and slanting up the south side.

It is just a brief pull onto the commencement of the well named Sharp Edge, considered by many to be superior to its great rival on Helvellyn. While not matching Striding Edge in extent, this razor edge demands more handling of rock, and induces a sense of exposure not experienced on Helvellyn's equivalent. There are no questions of route-finding, the famous knife-edge being an infallible and exhilarating guide. Those of a nervous disposition will take advantage, for the most part, of a well-worn path to the north below the edge proper, but when the spiky turrets cease, all must face a fascinating scramble up a benevolently tilted slab.

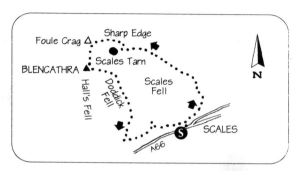

Above the slab the fun ends abruptly near the peak crowning Foule Crag, which with the summit itself, gives the mountain its undeniably descriptive name of Saddleback. Foule Crag's minor top is set back from the edge and rarely visited, rising a mere 50 or so feet above the saddle linking it with Blencathra's main summit. From here a much trodden path south across the eastern edge of the saddle will lead to Blencathra's meagre summit cairn, with the main ridge stretching away to the west. If crossing the crest of the broad saddle, the way passes a tiny tarn and a memorial cross of dazzling quartz stones.

The summit perches neatly above the remarkable southern face of the mountain, with the Hall's Fell ridge striking emphatically down from the very cairn. The panorama reveals an astonishing sweep of Lakeland filling the southern half of the picture. Derwentwater and Thirlmere represent the lakes, while most of the major fells are on show. Nothing, however, is more impressive than the dramatic downward scene where Hall's Fell divides the depths of Doddick Gill and Gate Gill. Blencathra's relative detachment from the bulk of the high fell country endows it with a better chance than most of escaping the low cloud that attaches itself to the tightly packed mountains. Additional attractions include the extensive skyline of the North Pennines beyond the Eden Valley.

Leave by retracing steps a short way east above the steep southern drop, and when the Sharp Edge path goes left, keep straight on the southern crest. The path descends gently above Doddick Gill to a platform at the onset of the Doddick Fell ridge, with Scales Fell continuing ahead. Turn right onto Doddick Fell, which provides a super descent, being neither too steep nor as worn as some of Blencathra's paths. Doddick Fell is a delightful scaled down version of Hall's Fell, proudly on display as the adjacent ridge. Doddick Fell, however, substitutes heathery rambling for its neighbour's more demanding scrambling. The path leads unfailingly down to the intake wall, where turn left on the path which quickly runs on to encounter Scaley Beck. A mini-scramble either side presents a sting in the tail, a last reminder of Sharp Edge! Exercise some caution at this obstacle, beyond which the path leads back to the gate at the start.

The upper section of Sharp Edge

SUMMITS	
BLENCATHRA	2848ft/868m

START Threlkeld   **Grid ref.** NY 318256

DISTANCE 4 miles/6½km   **ASCENT** 2362ft/720m

ORDNANCE SURVEY MAPS
1:50,000 - Landranger 90   1:25,000 - Outdoor Leisure 5

ACCESS Start from the village centre. National Park car park up Blease Road, off the main street. Served by Penrith-Keswick buses and seasonal Keswick-Patterdale and Keswick-Mungrisdale services.

No Lakeland mountain puts its goods in the shop window to better effect than Blencathra: the arresting profile of its magnificent south front could stop anything in its tracks. With such a wealth of routes there is no excuse for treading the same ground twice, although inevitably certain routes stand out above others. The celebrated Sharp Edge is the ascent route of WALK 22, while this climb utilises Hall's Fell, central and finest of the southern ridges.

Three slim spurs emanate from Blencathra's summit skyline, each broadening considerably before embracing the valley floor. This handsome trio of Gategill Fell, Hall's Fell and Doddick Fell shelter two steep-sided gills, while the broad shoulders of Blease Fell and Scales Fell sweep round to enclose the package, each ushering another impressive gill in with it. This walk ascends by a steep central ridge, savours a skyline walk, then descends a gentler outer flank.

S The village of Threlkeld enjoys a special affinity with this strong, silent type watching over it, and has a couple of welcoming hostelries awaiting the return of Blencathra-bound walkers. From the car park on Blease Road take the grassy way rising from the adjacent open area. This quickly narrows and rises with Blease Gill, crossing it and continuing up to a gate onto the base of the open fell. The ridge

85

immediately above is Gategill Fell. Turn sharp right through another gate, and follow the faint path along the top side of the intake wall. Already there are good views over much of northern Lakeland: the former Threlkeld Quarry is prominent across the valley, with Clough Head rising behind, the northern outpost of the Helvellyn range.

Towards the end the Hall's Fell ridge reveals itself, climbing infallibly to the summit, fittingly known as Hallsfell Top. Reaching the environs of Gate Gill, the drama begins to unfold, this rugged side valley showing remains of lead mining activity, and carving a direct line down from the summit peak high above. Cross the beck and bear left on the main path, which immediately sets about its direct ascent.

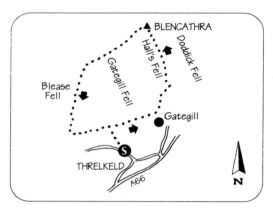

Initially steep but well graded, the fun starts promptly at the commencement, on a knoll, of the ridge proper. At this point a real sense of the mountain's ridges is gained, as Doddick Fell and Scales Fell enter the picture alongside. With near-vertical views down into Gate Gill and Doddick Gill, the narrowing ridge becomes a transport of delights, with a succession of rock towers, most incorporating an easy angled side. While an alternative lower level path has been worn, it would be criminal to use it unless conditions dictate otherwise. Opportunities to climb, with relative ease, a rocky spine such as this are few and far between, and here, more than ever, it's not just a matter of getting there, but also how you get there. The icing on the cake awaits at the top, for the ridge remains robust to the very end, abruptly and unexpectedly terminating at a sprawling cairn that reveals itself as the true summit of the mountain.

Disappointment that a classic climb has ended is tempered by the satisfaction of the panorama thus revealed, although nothing is more impressive than the dramatic downward scene comprising Hall's Fell and the depths of Doddick Gill. To the north is the hitherto unseen rolling country of the Skiddaw Forest, with Skiddaw and the Caldbeck Fells a perfect antidote to Blencathra's narrow edges. Blencathra's relative detachment from the bulk of the high fell country endows it with a better chance than most of escaping the low cloud that attaches itself to the tightly packed mountains. Additional attractions include the extensive skyline of the North Pennines beyond the Eden Valley.

Having gained such height, the benefits can be reaped by enjoying a near-level walk west above the broken southern face to the peak of Gategill Fell Top (2792ft/851m). Advance further to drop gently to the crest of Knowe Crags, on Blease Fell (2637ft/804m). Here the craggy front finally abates, and after a few faint yards a clear path resurrects itself to begin the descent. This is the ideal descent route for savouring the big views ahead, with so much of Lakeland on show including two of its waters, Thirlmere and Derwentwater. Remain on this broad path which undertakes a steeper section before easing out as a grassy way.

A good part of the way down, a distinct grooved way is encountered. Here the main path turns left to join it, slanting gently down to reveal a bird's-eye view of the village. The sunken way succumbs to a steeper path slanting down to the base of the fell. During this final stage Blease Gill and Gategill Fell make an inspiring pairing. The path joins the intake wall beneath a tiny plantation. Pass through the kissing-gate and follow the wall the few minutes back to the point where the fell was gained, and return back down in the company of Blease Gill.

Blencathra from Castlerigg Stone Circle

SUMMITS
HIGH RIGG   1171ft/357m

START *Legburthwaite*   **Grid ref.** *NY 317196*

DISTANCE *5 miles/8km*   **ASCENT** *900ft/275m*

ORDNANCE SURVEY MAPS
1:50,000 - Landranger 90   1:25,000 - Outdoor Leisure 5

ACCESS *Start from the North West Water car park on the B5322, half a mile north of its junction with the A591. The main road is served by Keswick-Windermere buses.*

High Rigg is a curious name for a fell that struggles for breathing space above the thousand foot contour, but such is its isolation that it appears far loftier, especially in winter raiment. Craggy outcrops typical of the junior fells add greatly to the appeal of this absorbing traverse of one of Lakeland's unsung miniature fells.

S From the car park do not rejoin the road but cross to the gated road that links the two classified roads, and turn left for the A591. Just over the bridge to the right a stile admits to the southern tip of High Rigg's elongated tract of upland. Break off the main path at once by taking the path climbing left to commence an enjoyable traverse of the ridge. The only steeper climbing comes in this initial pull, beyond which undulating terrain is the order of the day. Looking back, Thirlmere quickly appears, and there is no better vantage point for appraising nearby Castle Rock, to the right.

On the cairned top of Wren Crag the entire ridgewalk appears ahead, though the fascinating path will prove to meander between, rather than over, every bump. Blencathra rises majestically beyond St. John's in the Vale, straight across which are the craggy lower flanks and ravines of Clough Head and the Dodds. A slight drop is made to a gateway in a narrow defile, then a stroll across the top of Long Band leads towards a fence coming up from the left. It is crossed by a stile from where the path surprisingly heads away, before swinging right to rise to a brow beyond which a prominent wall junction is seen in a depression ahead. From the stile at the junction a green path rises up, and when the wall parts company the summit of the fell is in full view only a short distance farther ahead.

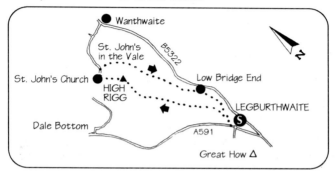

A cairn on a rocky knoll marks the summit. With deep valleys as a moat, High Rigg is surrounded by loftier fells, with the northern giants of Skiddaw and Blencathra both well placed. The latter is the more spectacular, but on this occasion it is rivalled by the craggy wall of Clough Head across St. John's in the Vale. While much else is in view, the hause in which stands the church of St. John's in the Vale is not. It is the key to the return, and is only ten minutes distant. Descend the rocks immediately below the summit to a green path heading north from the depression, which quickly becomes clearer in bracken. As the church appears a steeper drop leads down to a kissing-gate, where pass round to the left of the buildings to gain the narrow road.

Turning right on the road past the Diocesan youth centre and the squat church, a bridleway heads off to the right. It maintains an infallible course along the base of the fell, looking across the vale to Clough Head's flanks. A splendid green track virtually throughout its length, the actual bridleway turns off left when level with arched Sosgill Bridge. A footpath keeps up the running though, on beneath some new plantings before reaching the farm at Low Bridge End (refreshments). Passing along the back of it, the green path resumes as before to become sandwiched between the beck and the craggy fell. Rising away, it finishes impressively above the beck as it curves round to the roadside stile where the walk began.

SUMMITS	
CLOUGH HEAD	2382ft/726m
GREAT DODD	2812ft/857m
WATSON'S DODD	2588ft/789m
STYBARROW DODD	2766ft/843m

START Legburthwaite   **Grid ref.** NY 317196

DISTANCE 10 miles/16km   **ASCENT** 2900ft/884m

ORDNANCE SURVEY MAPS
1:50,000 - Landranger 90   1:25,000 - Outdoor Leisure 5

ACCESS Start from the North West Water car park on the B5322, half a mile north of its junction with the A591. The main road is served by Keswick-Windermere buses.

An enjoyable valley pre-amble sets the scene for a high level grassy stroll, with a surprisingly easy ascent and descent.

S North West Water's Legburthwaite car park stands sheltered in trees, and also has toilets and a picnic area. It is overlooked by the magnificent Castle Rock, which stands at the base of Watson's Dodd yet is not seen when actually upon the fell. Leave by a small gate at the far end onto a narrow back lane. Go left on this to the A591, and turn right over Smaithwaite Bridge. At once take a ladder-stile on the right, and within minutes the path forks, Take the upper one, which forks again just beyond. This time remain on the lower one, which runs a delightful course along the steep lower flank of High Rigg. Ahead, Blencathra increasingly fills the scene.

Through the trees the path joins the beck briefly, before running on with the wall to Low Bridge End Farm. The path is deflected up around the back of the buildings, and at the far end it forks. Go through the gate on the right to rejoin the beck, which now leads unfailingly downstream to the lovely arch of Sosgill Bridge. Remain on the bank beyond the bridge until the beck swings away, then keep straight on the fence-side. As St. John's in the Vale opens out, the profile of Lonscale Fell also impresses ahead, while to the right are the remains of Bramcrag Quarry and the ravine of Sandbed Gill.

The path traces a sunken way for some time before waymarks send it left to meet the returning sunken way at a stile. Resume, and when the fence turns away keep straight on and over a drain to the next stile. Clough Head now starts to appear, set back from lower crags to the right. Another drain is crossed on an improving green way which runs to the white-walled Bridge House, the beck returning for charming company. Joining the drive this leads out above the beck to join a back road, though the last section is short-cut on a path by the beck. At the road turn right, crossing Wanthwaite Bridge and rising to the B5322.

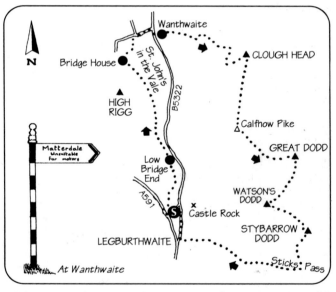

Go right 100 yards to a roadsign pointing the way to *Matterdale, unsuitable for motors.* This is the Old Coach Road, an historic route between St. John's in the Vale and Dockray. The rough road climbs left of the farm, with the extensive spoil of Hilltop Quarries up above. As the road swings left the right-hand wall ends, and a stile in the fence gives access to the defunct workings. A short pull through spoil heaps leads up to a broad green track. Only fifty yards to the right a parallel track, the bed of a former mineral line, is transferred to, immediately above. From here a path commences a steep climb through plantings near the edge of a large old quarry. From a stile at the top a thin path climbs to a ladder-stile over a wall onto the open fell. This makes a good place to halt and look back to what is already a fine panorama of the north-western fells. To the north, the white houses of Threlkeld nestle beneath Blencathra's majestic frontage.

Unerringly and effortlessly a sunken way rises above the wall, its twists and turns outwitting the gradient. This splendid old sledgate only expires on entering an amphitheatre above Wanthwaite Crags to the right and below the craggy scree slopes under Clough Head's summit. As the sunken section ends advance up a grassy way to a cairn, which sends a fainter cairned way up the now stony steeper slopes. Keep an eye out for the penultimate cairn where the path swings sharp right to commence a slanting rake up the rough flank. It remains totally clear throughout, traversing the face and rising with ease to emerge at a cairn that marks a sudden end to the rough terrain. At this point Great Dodd appears, with Helvellyn beyond. The way to Clough Head's summit is a pathless stroll up the grass slopes to the left.

A shelter and an Ordnance Survey column occupy this northern outpost of the Helvellyn range, and the ultimate reward is found in two major aspects of the view. Firstly the prospect of Blencathra, a classic mountain study, while westwards is a succession of delights, with the Vale of Keswick featuring both Bassenthwaite Lake and Derwentwater. The foot of the latter is backed by the shapely outlines of the Grasmoor group, while continuing further round, Scafell Pike and its considerable supporting cast acquit themselves admirably.

Turning away, the dome of Great Dodd fills the ridge, and a path heads southwards to immediately reveal Thirlmere below. This grassy stroll gives ample opportunity to savour the western panorama before reaching Calfhow Pike just across the saddle. This solid tor makes an intriguing halfway point, sitting uneasily in its grassy surround. The climb to Great Dodd is uneventful, a steady pull at the top of which the path fades on the final steeper section. Continue up to find the summit cairn sat alone on the broad domed top. A useful shelter stands 150 yards to its south-east. This fell of immense girth displays few distinguishing features, and in common with its fellow Dodds is territory for the walker who prefers long strides and distant horizons. The two contrasting panoramas are of a succession of ridges westwards, and eastwards the unbroken chain of Pennine heights, far beyond the sprawl of no-man's-land marking the boundary of this corner of Lakeland.

Next major summit along the ridge is Stybarrow Dodd, a similarly benign giant. Heading south, a good path quickly forms from which to enjoy the Helvellyn skyline ahead. The ridge dog-legs between these two Dodds, and in the saddle the path forks. There are in fact two direct options, while a longer path keeps to the true watershed by going right, on the broad ridge out to the large cairn on Watson's Dodd. This minor top links the two major Dodds, and its protruding position well out to the west results in what is the best picture of the Helvellyn range from the actual ridge itself.

The climb to Stybarrow Dodd is a very brief one, and, inevitably, the path performs its party piece by marginally skirting the summit. When the path levels out, rise left for two minutes to the highest point. A cairn is found incorporating an upright slate slab, a boundary stone that formerly stood some distance away. Extensive, rather than exciting views are the order of the day. The top end of a crumbling wall is found just to the north-east, offering a modicum of shelter if it be needed.

Return to the path which continues along to a cairn on the south-west top, where it briefly fades. Here the way turns south, quickly reappearing for a rapid descent to the top of Sticks Pass. During these few minutes there is a nice cameo of the head of Ullswater and its environs down to the left. Note that it is not necessary to drop to the summit of the pass, for from the south-west top's cairn one can simply slant south-west down grassy slopes to intercept the path as it crosses this broad shoulder of the fell.

Turning right, a good path keeps exclusively to Stybarrow Dodd's shoulder, until an old sheepfold overlooks a change of character as a steeper drop is made by the ravine of Stanah Gill. Still mostly grassy, the way drops down into bracken, and at the bottom corner the path turns to bridge the gill in a truly lovely setting. Across, a lower gate sees the path down a pasture to a step-stile by a water cut, then down to a ladder-stile onto a back road. Just below, it meets the main road junction at Legburthwaite. Turn right for a few minutes on the 'B' road, passing a youth hostel (the former school) and a Mission Room of 1881 before reaching the car park.

TABLE OF SUMMITS

	FELL	FEET	METRES	
1	SKIDDAW **M**	3054	931	....
2	GREAT GABLE **M**	2949	899	....
3	BLENCATHRA **M**	2848	868	....
4	GREAT DODD	2812	857	....
5	STYBARROW DODD	2766	843	....
6	GREEN GABLE	2628	801	....
7	GRISEDALE PIKE **M**	2595	791	....
8	Watson's Dodd #	2588	789	....
9	ALLEN CRAGS	2575	785	....
10	GLARAMARA	2569	783	....
11	DALE HEAD **M**	2470	753	....
12	CARL SIDE	2447	746	....
13	HOBCARTON CRAG •	2425	739	....
14	ROBINSON **M**	2418	737	....
15	LONG SIDE	2408	734	....
16	HINDSCARTH	2385	727	....
17	CLOUGH HEAD	2382	726	....
18	GLARAMARA SOUTH TOP •	2365	721	....
19	BOWSCALE FELL	2303	702	....
20	Ullock Pike #	2270	692	....
21	BANNERDALE CRAGS	2241	683	....
22	Bakestall #	2208	673	....
23	SCAR CRAGS	2205	672	....
24	CARROCK FELL	2175	663	....
25	HIGH PIKE	2159	658	....
26	HIGH SPY	2142	653	....
27	BASE BROWN	2119	646	....
28	CAUSEY PIKE	2090	637	....
29	DOVENEST TOP •	2073	632	....
30	Ard Crags	1906	581	....
31	Maiden Moor	1889	576	....
32	Outerside	1863	568	....
33	Knott Rigg	1824	556	....
34	Lord's Seat **M**	1811	552	....
35	Meal Fell	1804	550	....
36	Great Cockup	1726	526	....
37	Barf	1536	468	....
38	Great Crag	1496	456	....
39	Barrow	1492	455	....
40	Catbells	1480	451	....
41	Stile End •	1466	447	....
42	Brund Fell (Grange Fell)	1363	415	....
43	King's How (Grange Fell) •	1286	392	....
44	Walla Crag	1243	379	....
45	Latrigg	1207	368	....
46	Sale Fell	1178	359	....
47	High Rigg **M**	1171	357	....
48	Castle Crag	951	290	....

KEY

For walkers who like their hills to be classified:
UPPER CASE - 2000ft fells with at least 100ft/30m of re-ascent ('HEWITT')
\# - minor 2000ft fells   • - non 'WAINWRIGHT' fells
M - fells with at least 500ft/150m of re-ascent ('MARILYN')

LOG OF THE WALKS

WALK	DATE	NOTES
1		
2		
3		
4		
5		
6		
7		
8		
9		
10		
11		
12		
13		
14		
15		
16		
17		
18		
19		
20		
21		
22		
23		
24		
25		

INDEX
Summits and other principle features
Walk number refers; Start points in bold